THINGS YOU OUGHT TO KNOW
GAME TIME

Terry O'Brien is an esteemed academician and an ardent quiz aficionado. He is keenly interested in kindling the quizzing instinct in people and an aptitude to develop the 3Rs of learning: Read, Record, and Recall. He is a trainers' instructor and a motivational speaker. He has penned many books. He is very well known for his flair for speaking and his articulating abilities in writing.

Bestsellers by the Author

CATEGORY I

Language skills for all age groups from class 3 onwards: The Little Red Book series.

CATEGORY II

For beginners: *A Child's First Dictionary* (The Little Red Book series).

CATEGORY III

To develop a love for reading among schoolchildren and also for adults, a collection of the best stories by renowned writers: The Masterpieces of World Fiction series.

CATEGORY IV

For developing quiz instinct and general awareness: The Fun Fact series—*Fun with Numbers, Fun with Riddles,* etc.; *A2Z Quiz Book; The Book of Firsts and Lasts.*

CATEGORY V

Motivational books: *The Book of Virtues* and *The Book of Motivation.*

CATEGORY VI

For overall preparation and general awareness: *The Students' Companion.*

CATEGORY VII

Teachers' reference book: *A2Z Book of Word Origins.*

THINGS YOU OUGHT TO KNOW

GAME TIME

TERRY O' BRIEN

Published by
Rupa Publications India Pvt. Ltd. 2016
7/16, Ansari Road, Daryaganj
New Delhi 110 002

Sales Centres:
Allahabad Bengaluru Chennai
Hyderabad Jaipur Kathmandu
Kolkata Mumbai

Copyright © Terry O'Brien 2016

The views and opinions expressed in this book are the author's own and the facts are as reported by him/her which have been verified to the extent possible, and the publishers are not in any way liable for the same.

All rights reserved.
No part of this publication may be reproduced, transmitted, or stored in a retrieval system, in any form or by any means, electronic, mechanical, photocopying, recording or otherwise, without the prior permission of the publisher.

ISBN : 978-81-291-3792-0

First impression 2016

10 9 8 7 6 5 4 3 2 1

The moral right of the author has been asserted.

Typeset by Innovative Processors, New Delhi

Printed by Shree Maitrey Printech Pvt. Ltd., Noida

This book is sold subject to the condition that it shall not, by way of trade or otherwise, be lent, resold, hired out, or otherwise circulated, without the publisher's prior consent, in any form of binding or cover other than that in which it is published.

Contents

Preface vii
I. Board & Card Games 1
II. Dungeons & Dragons 108
III. Scrabble 112
IV. Risk 116
V. The Game of Life 119
VI. Clue 122
VII. Monopoly 126
VIII. Puzzles 132
IX. Playground & Backyard Games 137
X. Video Games 142
XI. Traditional Games of India 155

Preface

Games were not just games; they were designed in such a way that one can develop skills like logical thinking, building strategy, concentration, basic mathematics, aiming, and a lot more. Games act as learning aids. They teach us many things such as learn to win and lose, develop sensory skills, count, add, improve motor skills, identify colour, improve co-ordination and finally to have fun!

Since the beginning of time, man has theorised about the meaning of strategy. Some said it is an art; others it is a science. Games provide a wonderful platform for intergenerational understanding, strategy and learning. Kids often take the lead in showing their parents what they know in the game—they are the experts!

Indeed, games give both parents and their children a chance to interact and learn together. Games add to a repertoire of skills and entertainment.

This book provides information on the very essence of games—its rules, strategy and, of course, its roots and origin. **Things You Should Know: Game Time** contains facts that will inform, amaze and entertain. The bottom line is that you will learn through fun.

1
BOARD & CARD GAMES

Playing Cards

- ❖ On early Egyptian playing cards, there were symbols of Cups, Coins and Swords. But there were no Crowns.
- ❖ The very first appearance of playing cards goes back to the country where paper was invented, i.e. China.
- ❖ Playing cards appeared in Europe in the late 14th century, and very quickly got banned. This was because of their use for gambling.
- ❖ Hearts, Diamonds, Clubs and Spades have been varied.
- ❖ In Spain, they opted to use Coins, Cups, Swords and Clubs (items that are still found on their cards today).

- The court cards (Jack, Queen and King) in a standard US deck are based on real people from history. This practice started in France; although not all court cards depict French people.

- The King of Spades is based on King David (of Biblical fame); the King of Diamonds Julius Caesar; and the Queen of Hearts Judith (also Biblical).

- Ace of Spades is the card that traditionally bears the insignia of the company which produces the deck of cards.

- Before it was known as the Jack, the court card below the Queen was called 'The Knave'.

- The Joker didn't actually get introduced into the standard deck until the late 19th century. It first appeared in American decks to allow for an extra trump card in the game of Euchre.

- USPC (United States Playing Card Company), founded in 1867, has become one of the world's largest producers of playing card decks. It has produced an estimated 100 million decks of playing cards annually at the turn of the 21st century.

- In November 2007, Liu Fuchang set a new Guiness World Record for owning 11,000 individual decks of different playing cards.

✦✦✦✦✦✦

Battleship

- Battleship (also Battleships or Sea Battle) is a guessing game for two players.
- It is known worldwide as a pencil and paper game which dates back to World War I.
- Back then, it was called Broadsides—the game of naval strategy.
- It was published by various companies as a pad-and-pencil game in the 1930s, and was released as a plastic board game by Milton Bradley in 1967.
- On a Battleship game board, the highest letter is 'J'.
- There are three peg spaces in battleship's submarine piece.
- The 2010 updated version of Battleship includes islands.
- The game is played on four grids, two for each player.
- The grids are typically square—usually 10×10—and the individual squares in the grid are identified by letter and number.
- On one grid, the player arranges ships and records the shots by the opponent.
- On the other grid, the player records his/her own shots.
- Before the play begins, each player secretly arranges their ships on their primary grid.

- Each ship occupies a number of consecutive squares on the grid, arranged either horizontally or vertically.
- The number of squares for each ship is determined by the type of the ship.

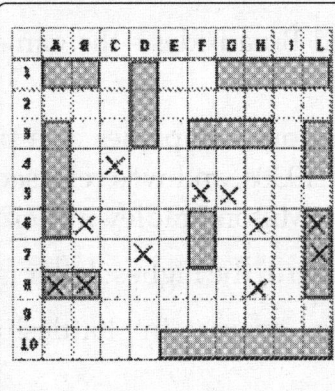

A MAP of one player's ships and the hits against them, from a game in progress. The grey boxes are the ships placed by the player, and the cross marks show the squares that their opponent has fired upon. The player would be tracking the success of their own shots in a separate grid.

Boggle

- The verb boggled or boggling means to overwhelm or bewilder, as with the magnitude, complexity, or abnormality.
- Boggle is a word game designed by Allan Turoff.
- The game was originally distributed by Parker Brothers.
- The game is played using a plastic grid of lettered dice, in which players attempt to find words in sequences of adjacent letters.

- The game begins by shaking a covered tray of 16 cubic dice, each with a different letter printed on each of its sides.
- The dice settle into a 4×4 tray so that only the top letter of each cube is visible.
- After they settle into the grid, a three-minute sand timer is started and all players simultaneously begin the main phase of play.
- Each player searches for words that can be constructed from the letters of sequentially adjacent cubes, where 'adjacent' cubes are those horizontally, vertically and diagonally neighbouring.
- Words must be at least three letters long, may include singular and plural (or other derived forms) separately, but may not use the same letter cube more than once per word.
- Each player records all the words he or she finds by writing on a private sheet of paper.
- After three minutes have elapsed, all players must immediately stop writing and the game enters the scoring phase.
- In the scoring phase, each player reads off his or her list of discovered words.
- If two or more players wrote the same word, it is removed from all players' lists.
- Any player may challenge the validity of a word, in which case a previously nominated dictionary is used to verify or refute it.

- For all words remaining after duplicates have been eliminated, points are awarded based on the length of the word.
- The winner is the player whose point total is highest, with any ties typically broken by count of long words.
- One cube is printed with 'QU'. This is because Q is nearly always followed by U in English words, and if there were a Q in Boggle, it would be challenging to use if a U did not, by chance, appear next to it.
- For the purpose of scoring, 'QU' counts as two letters: squid would score two points (for a five-letter word) despite being formed from a chain of only four cubes.
- The North American National Scrabble Association publishes the Official Scrabble Players Dictionary (OSPD), which is also suitable for Boggle.
- This dictionary includes all variant forms of words up to eight letters in length.
- A puzzle book entitled 100 Boggle Puzzles (Improve Your Game) offering 100 game positions was published in the UK in 2003.
- The bottom line: race against each other to change the four-letter word on the table.
- Change 'game' to 'fame', 'fate', 'late'. Be the first to get rid of all of your cards and win the game!

❖ Double your fun with the free Shuffle app: activate bonus letter cards and lock out the other players so you can play faster!

Boggle

A grid of Boggle cubes and a sand timer

Manufacturer(s)	Parker Brothers (now Hasbro)
Designer(s)	Allan Turoff
Publication date	1972; 43 years ago
Genre(s)	Word game Dice game
Players	2+
Age range	8+
Setup time	1 minute
Skill(s) required	Language
Material(s) required	Paper and writing utensils

Candy Land

❖ Candy Land is a simple racing board game.

- ❖ The game requires no reading and minimal counting skills, making it suitable for young children.
- ❖ Due to the design of the game, there is no strategy involved—players are never required to make choices, just follow directions.
- ❖ The winner is predetermined by the shuffle of the cards.
- ❖ The race is woven around a storyline about finding King Kandy, the lost king of Candy Land.
- ❖ The board consists of a winding, linear track made of 134 spaces, mostly red, green, blue, yellow, orange or purple.
- ❖ The remaining pink spaces are named locations such as Candy Cane Forest and Gum Drop Mountain, or characters such as Queen Frostine and Gramma Nutt.
- ❖ The game was designed in 1949 by Eleanor Abbott, while she was recovering from polio in San Diego, California.
- ❖ The game was bought by Milton Bradley Company (now owned by Hasbro) and first published in 1949.
- ❖ Hasbro produces several versions of the game and treats it as a brand. For example, they market Candy Land puzzles, a travel version, a personal computer game, and a handheld electronic version.

Candy Land

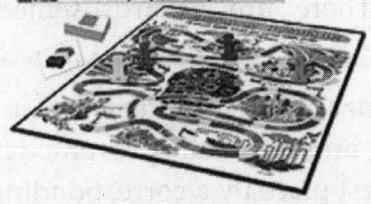

Publisher(s)	Hasbro and Winning Moves
Players	2 to 4
Setup time	< 3 minutes
Playing time	< 15 to 21 minutes
Random chance	Complete
Skill(s) required	Colour recognition

Mille Bornes

- ❖ The premise of Mille Bornes is that the players are in a road race.

- ❖ Each race—or hand—is usually 700 miles (or kilometers) long, but the first player to complete that distance exactly has the option to declare an extension in which case the race becomes 1,000 miles.

- Other times the game is played up to 1000 miles first, and then the first player to complete that distance has the option to declare an 'extension' for 1,200 miles.
- Mille Bornes is played with a special deck of cards. There are hazard, remedy, safety and distance cards.
- Each hazard is corrected by a corresponding remedy, and is actually prevented from happening in the first place by a corresponding safety.
- The target distance is reached by playing distance cards.
- Six cards are dealt to each player at the start of Mille Bornes.

Mille Bornes	

Modern edition	
Manufacturer(s)	Winning Moves
Designer(s)	Edmond Dujardin, born in Ecuador and raised in France
Illustrator(s)	Joseph Le Callennec

Publication date	1954
Genre(s)	Take That
Language(s)	English / French
Skill(s) required	Medium
Media type	Cards

Reversi/Othello

- ❖ The board game Reversi was invented in the 19th century, allegedly by either John W. Mollett or Lewis Waterman.

- ❖ The game was rechristened Othello in the 1970s by Goro Hasegawa and marketed by the Japanese game company Tsukuda Original, then subsequently introduced to the American market by Pressman.

- ❖ Described as taking 'a minute to learn, a lifetime to master,' the 2-player game Othello requires strategy to outflank your opponent in order to capture and flip his or her pieces.

- ❖ The game of Othello starts with four pieces in the centre of the board.

- ❖ In Othello, the dark makes the first move.

- ❖ In Othello, pieces placed in the corners cannot be flipped.

Reversi

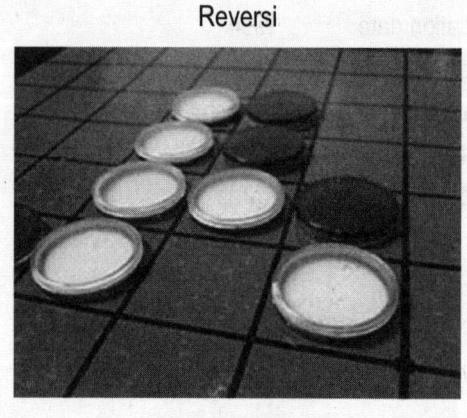

Years active	Since 1883
Genre(s)	Board game
	Abstract strategy game
Players	2
Age range	5+ years
Setup time	< 10 seconds
Playing time	5 to 60 minutes
Random chance	None

Pente

- The name of the popular game Pente means five in Greek.

- Pente is a strategy board game for two or more players, created in 1977 by Gary Gabrel, a dishwasher at Hideaway Pizza, in Stillwater, Oklahoma.

- Customers played Pente at Hideaway Pizza on checkerboard tablecloths while waiting for their orders to arrive.
- Pente is based on the Japanese game ninuki-renju, a variant of renju or gomoku that is played on a Go board of 19 x 19 intersections with white and black stones.
- Like renju and ninuki-renju, Pente allows captures, but Pente added a new opening rule.
- In the 19th century, gomoku was introduced to Britain where it was known as Go Bang (borrowed from Japanese 'goban', meaning 'go board').
- Pente is a registered trademark of Hasbro for strategy game equipment.
- Hasbro ceased distribution of Pente in 1993.
- It later licensed the game to Winning Moves, a classic games publisher that resurrected the game in 2004.
- The 2004 version includes 4 extra stones called power stones that can be played in the Pente Plus version.
- The players alternate in placing stones of their colour on free intersections, with White always assuming the opening move. The players aim to align five stones of the same colour suite in vertical, horizontal or diagonal lines.

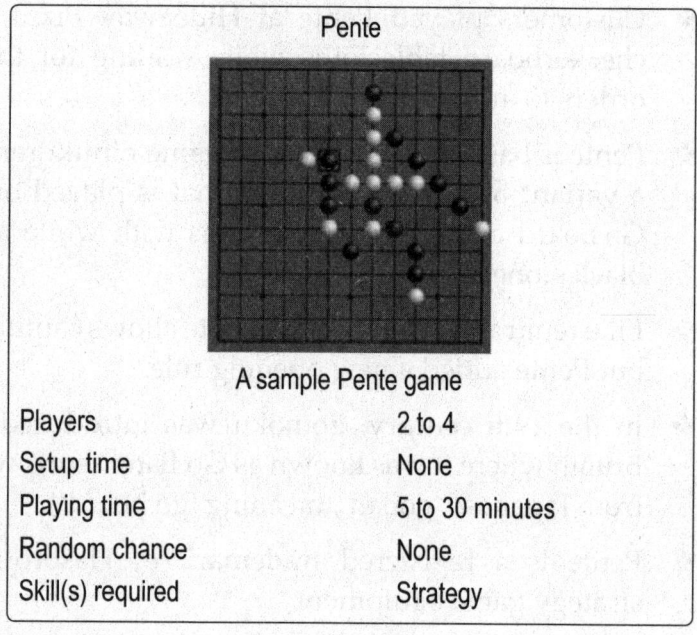

Players	2 to 4
Setup time	None
Playing time	5 to 30 minutes
Random chance	None
Skill(s) required	Strategy

Pokemon

- ❖ The Pokémon Trading Card Game is a collectible card game with a goal similar to a Pokémon battle in the video game series.

- ❖ Players use Pokémon cards, with individual strengths and weaknesses, in an attempt to defeat their opponent by 'knocking out' his or her Pokémon cards.

- ❖ The game was first published in North America by Wizards of the Coast in 1999.

- With the release of Pokémon Ruby and Sapphire Game Boy Advance video games, The Pokémon Company took back the card game from Wizards of the Coast and started publishing the cards themselves.
- The Expedition expansion introduced the Pokémon-e Trading Card Game, where the cards (for the most part) were compatible with the Nintendo e-Reader.
- Nintendo discontinued its production of e-Reader compatible cards with the release of EX FireRed & LeafGreen.
- In 1998, Nintendo released a Game Boy Colour version of the trading card game in Japan; Pokémon Trading Card Game was subsequently released to the US and Europe in 2000.
- The game included digital version cards from the original set of cards and the first two expansions (Jungle and Fossil), as well as several cards exclusive to the game. A Japan-exclusive sequel was released in 2001.
- The Pokémon Trading Card game first entered the Japanese market in 1996.
- You can draw seven cards at the beginning of a basic game of Pokémon.

Sorry

- ❖ Sorry is a board game that is based on the ancient Cross and Circle game Pachisi.
- ❖ Players try to travel around the board with their pieces faster than any other player.
- ❖ Originally manufactured by BCM (British Card Manufacturers) in England and now by Hasbro, Sorry is marketed for two to four players, ages six through adult.
- ❖ The game title Sorry comes from the many ways in which a player can negate the progress of another, while issuing an apologetic 'Sorry!'
- ❖ A classic edition of Sorry is currently produced in the US by Winning Moves.
- ❖ The earliest variation of today's Sorry can be traced back to England.
- ❖ William Henry Storey of Southend-on-Sea filed for a patent.
- ❖ Sorry was registered as a trademark on 21 May 1929.

- Early games were manufactured by BCM (British Card Manufacturers).
- Sorry was adopted by Parker Brothers in 1934.
- Hasbro now publishes it, as they purchased Parker Brothers in 1991.
- Each player chooses four pawns of one colour and one player is selected to play first.
- Each player, in turn, draws one card from the stack and follows its instructions.
- To begin the game, all of a player's four pawns are restricted to Start; only a 1 or 2 card can release them to the rest of the board. Playing a 1 or a 2 places a pawn on the space directly outside of start; playing a 2 does not entitle the pawn to a second space.
- The Relaxation Start: When a young player is playing especially when learning the game of Sorry, a Relaxation is offered in allowing one of their pawns to be placed on their Track-Start-Space. This means they don't get bored before they even start, in that they feel a part of things rather than the tedium of waiting for a 1 or a 2, which can be a bit wearisome even for experienced players.
- A player can jump over any other pawn, landing on the square indicated by the card. However, two pawns cannot occupy the same square.
- A pawn that lands on a square occupied by another 'bumps' that pawn back to its own Start.

THINGS YOU OUGHT TO KNOW: GAME TIME

- ❖ Players cannot bump their own pawns back to Start. If the only way to complete a move would result in a player bumping himself/herself, the pawns remain in place and the player loses his or her turn.

- ❖ If a pawn lands at the start of a slide (except those of its own colour) by direct movement or as the result of a switch with the 11 card or a Sorry card, it immediately moves to the last square of the slide.

- ❖ All pawns anywhere on the slide are sent back to their respective Starts.

- ❖ The last five squares before home are the 'safety zone'.

- ❖ Access is limited to those pawns of the same colour.

- ❖ Pawns inside the zone are immune to being replaced by an opponent's pawn with an 11 or a Sorry card.

- ❖ However, a pawn is vulnerable to being forcibly moved backward out of the safety zone.

- ❖ Forced backward moves can cause a pawn to exit the zone. Also, you cannot move your pawn backwards and forwards and count it as a space, no matter what card you have, it is not allowed to move backwards and forwards.

- ❖ Each player gets four pawns in a game of Sorry.

- ❖ The numbers six and nine are the two numbers, that are not featured on the cards in a game of Sorry.

- One can move back one space, besides moving ten spaces forward, when you draw a ten card in Sorry.

Sorry!

Older edition

Publisher(s)	BCM Parker Brothers Waddingtons Winning Moves
Players	2 to 4
Setup time	1 to 5 minutes
Random chance	High (Cards)
Skill(s) required	Counting, Tactics, Strategy, Probability

Stratego

- Stratego is a classic board game by Milton Bradley, played on a 10×10 grid.

- Players each have an army of pieces with hidden values, which they move around to try to capture the flag of the other player.

The basic rules of Stratego

Players: 2

Components: 1 board, containing a 10×10 grid of squares, with two impassable areas in the middle. 80 pieces, 40 for each player, including one flag, six bombs, a spy, and military pieces ranging in value from 1 to 9.

Goal: To capture the opposing flag by moving onto it with one of your pieces.

Setup: Each player takes all the pieces of one colour. Secretly arrange your pieces so their values are facing you, and your opponent only sees the blank backs. Set up your side of the board by placing one piece in each space in the back four rows.

Once both sides are set up, choose a starting player and begin.

How to Play:

- On your turn, you must move one of your pieces.
- Flags and bombs are immobile, and can never be moved.
- Other pieces may move one space in any of the

four directions (not diagonally), so long as they land in either an empty space or a space containing an opposing piece.

- ❖ The two water formations in the middle of the board are impassable obstacles, and not valid spaces.
- ❖ Scouts (marked with a 9 in the original edition) may move any number of spaces in a straight line, but must stop on the space with the first enemy piece they encounter.
- ❖ When a piece lands on the same space as another piece (referred to as 'attacking'), the values of the two pieces are compared.
- ❖ The piece with the worse rank (higher number, in the original edition) is defeated and removed from the board.
- ❖ In the case of a tie, when a piece attacks an opposing piece of the same value, both pieces are removed from the board.
- ❖ If a piece attacks a bomb, the attacking piece is immediately defeated, unless the attacker was a Miner (marked with an 8 in the original edition). In that case, the bomb is defeated.
- ❖ If the Spy (S) attacks the opposing Marshall (marked with a 1 in the original edition), the Marshall is defeated. If the Spy attacks any other piece, or is attacked by any piece including the Marshall, the Spy is defeated.

- ❖ **Game End:**

  If you attack your opponent's flag with any piece, you win the game.

  If you cannot move a piece on your turn, you immediately lose the game.

- ❖ **Note:** Some newer editions of Stratego reverse the rankings, making higher numbers stronger instead of weaker, and using 10s as the Marshalls.

- ❖ Stratego Card Battle is the ultimate fast-paced attacking strategy card game. The game remains the same, a head-to-head battle to capture the enemy flag!

- ❖ With new and exciting rules to play by, Stratego Card Battle is ideal for new and loyal Stratego fans.

- ❖ Each player's 40 pieces in Stratego has six bombs.

- ❖ There are ten spaces wide in a Stratego board.

- ❖ Each Stratego player has only one flag.

- ❖ In Stratego, a Colonel is of higher rank than a Major.

- ❖ In Stratego, a Lieutenant is ranked higher than a Miner.

- ❖ In Stratego, a Captain is ranked higher than a Scout.

- ❖ The familiar version of Stratego was first published in The Netherlands.

Stratego

Genre(s)	Board game
	Strategy game
Players	2
Age range	8 and up
Setup time	2 to 10 minutes
Playing time	30 to 120 minutes
Random chance	None
Skill(s) required	Strategy, tactics, memory

Uno

- ❖ Uno was invented in 1971.
- ❖ Uno (Italian and Spanish for 'one') is an American card game which is played with a specially printed deck.
- ❖ The game was originally developed in 1971 by Merle Robbins in Reading, Ohio, a suburb of Cincinnati.

- ❖ It has been a Mattel product since 1992. The game's general principles put it into the Crazy Eights family of card games.
- ❖ A deck of English Uno cards from 1994 uses the older card design, where letters appear on the action cards instead of symbols.

Uno Cards Deck:

- ❖ The deck consists of 108 cards, of which there are twenty-five of each colour (red, green, blue and yellow), each colour having two of each rank except zero.
- ❖ The ranks in each colour are zero to nine.
- ❖ Skip, Draw Two and Reverse (the last three of these being classified as 'action cards').
- ❖ In addition, the deck contains four each of Wild and Wild Draw Four cards.
- ❖ To start a hand, seven cards are dealt out to each player, and the top card of the deck is flipped over and set aside to begin the discard pile.
- ❖ The player to the dealer's left plays first, unless the first card on the discard pile is an action or Wild card.
- ❖ On a player's turn, he/she must do one of the following:

    play a card matching the discard in colour, number or symbol,

    play a Wild card, or a playable Wild Draw Four card, or

    draw the top card of the deck.

- ❖ If a player chooses to draw the top card of the deck, and that card is playable (it matches the discard, or is a playable wild card), then the player may (but need not) immediately play that card.
- ❖ Play proceeds clockwise around the table.

UNO	
Type	Shedding-type
Players	2 to 10
Skill(s) required	Keeping important cards for later; knowing when to put them down, concealing your hand.
Age range	7+
Cards	108
Playing time	Normally up to 30 minutes but can go higher
Random chance	Easy

✦✦✦✦✦✦

Yahtzee

- ❖ Keep your eye on the cards! Collect dice cards to make classic combinations: 3 of a kind, 4 of a kind, small straight, large straight, full house and Yahtzee!
- ❖ Re-roll by discarding cards you don't need and taking a chance on new ones. But here's the twist: pit your hand against another player's. Score high and win the Combo card points.

- Includes 12 combo cards, 12 chance cards, 84 dice cards, 1 starter card, 1 reminder card, 1 combo sheet and instructions.
- Yahtzee is based on a similar game called Yacht.
- You get 30 points for a small straight in Yahtzee.
- You get 40 points for a large straight in Yahtzee.
- Technically, the minimum score is five in Yahtzee if you put five ones in Chance and 0s in every other box.
- 375 is the maximum Yahtzee score (without bonuses).
- There are two different dice sizes in Challenge Yahtzee.
- Showdown Yahtzee is a board game.

Present Yahtzee logo

Players	1+
Age range	8+
Playing time	30 minutes
Random chance	High
Skill(s) required	Luck, probability, strategy

✦✦✦✦✦✦

Ants in the Pants

- The name derives from an idiomatic English metaphor which asserts that nervous, fidgety people must have 'ants in their pants'.
- The English word 'antsy' (meaning nervous) also derives from this metaphor.
- Ants in the Pants is a children's tabletop game.
- The object of the game is to spring as many of your 'ants' as possible into the 'pants'. The game shares similarities with Tiddlywinks.
- Components consist of a free-standing pair of miniature (usually plastic), pants and several plastic ants.
- The ants are colour-coded—each player uses one colour of ants—and designed so that pressing the tail stores elastic potential energy. When the tail is pressed and released, the ants spring into the air.
- Some versions include cardboard characters which serve as backboards deflecting the ants into the pants.
- Plastic suspenders (or braces) are another common element, which serve as obstacles.
- Created by insect-theme game designer William H. Schaper, Ants in the Pants was originally published by his W. H. Schaper Mfg. Co. Inc. in 1969.
- In 1986, what was then known as Schaper Toys of Kusan Inc. was acquired by Tyco Toys, and

in the deal, Tyco sold the rights to four Schaper games (including Cootie and Ants in the Pants) to Hasbro's Milton Bradley division which currently manufactures the game.

Barrel of Monkeys

❖ Barrel of Monkeys is a toy game first created by Lakeside Toys in 1965.

❖ Original inventor was named Leonard Marks of Roslyn, New York.

❖ Today it is produced by the Milton Bradley Company within the Hasbro corporation.

❖ Milton Bradley's editions consist of a toy barrel in either blue, yellow, red or green. The barrel contains 12 monkeys but can hold 24, their colour usually corresponding to the barrel's colour.

- The instructions on the bottom of the barrel state: 'Dump monkeys onto table. Pick up one monkey by an arm. Hook other arm through a second monkey's arm. Continue making a chain. Your turn is over when a monkey is dropped.'
- In addition to these basic instructions, the barrel also contains instructions for playing alone or with two or more players.
- The first speed record for a standard 13 monkey barrel of monkeys game was officially recorded by 2:01:88 minutes and has yet to be beaten.
- Knock-offs come in additional colours under the name Monkeys in Barrel.
- Lakeside Toys originally developed the game using S-shaped hooks made from rubber and wire.
- They had intended to name it 'Barrel of Fun', but found that both that name and 'Barrel-O-Fun' were already being used by other game manufacturers.
- So the company decided to name their game after the related phrase 'more fun than a barrel of monkeys' and remodeled the S-hooks into plastic monkeys.
- Initially sold in a cardboard tube, Lakeside quickly produced a two-piece plastic barrel that completely replaced the cardboard version by 1968.
- You need twelve monkeys to hook together to win a game of Barrel of Monkeys.

Snakes and Ladders

- ❖ Snakes and Ladder or Chutes and Ladders is a metaphor for life.
- ❖ This game originated in India.
- ❖ The spaces in Snakes and Ladders are numbered.
- ❖ A Six in Snakes and Ladders allows you to move and then roll again.
- ❖ It is arguably the most philosophical of all children's board games.
- ❖ The game of Snakes and Ladders itself consists of a square board made up of 100 squares (ten squares by ten squares).
- ❖ To play, players roll a die and advance their token the rolled number of spaces, with the arrival at the end of the board—the hundredth square—being the ultimate goal.

- ❖ Snakes and Ladders is a metaphor for life itself by virtue of the fact that both the game and life have a definitive beginning and an end, with an inevitable progression from one to the other.

- ❖ And true to that metaphor, in the game (just as in life) there are 'ladders'—certain squares that advance a player forward a certain number of squares—and 'chutes'—certain squares that send a player back a certain number of squares.

- ❖ It is because of this underlying purpose that a vast amount of study has been devoted to this game.

- ❖ The game's 'snakes' and 'ladders' are a visual and physical representation of good and bad moral actions.

Snakes and Ladders

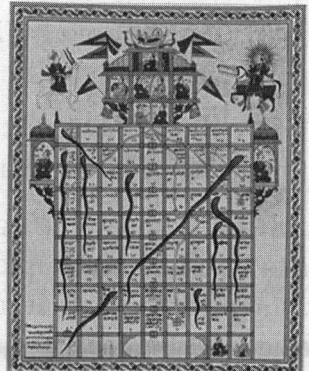

Game of Snakes and Ladders, gouache on cloth
(India, 19th century)

Genre(s)	Board game Race game Dice game
Players	2+
Age range	3+
Setup time	Negligible
Playing time	15 to 45 minutes
Random chance	Entirely
Skill(s) required	Counting, observation
Synonym(s)	Chutes and Ladders

Cootie

- Created by William Schaper in 1948, the game was launched in 1949 and sold millions in its first years.
- In 1973, Cootie was acquired by Tyco Toys, and in 1986, by Hasbro subsidiary Milton Bradley.
- The game of Cootie is a children's roll-and-move tabletop game for two to four players.
- The object of the original 1949 game is to be the first player to build a 'cootie' piece by piece from various plastic body parts that include a beehive-like body, a head, antennae, eyes, a coiled proboscis and six legs.
- Body parts are acquired following the player's roll of a die, with each number on the die corresponding to one of the body parts.

- ❖ The body corresponds to one, the head to two, the antennas (feelers) to three, the eye to four, the proboscis (mouth) to five, and the leg to six.
- ❖ The first part to be acquired must be the body, and then the head. All other body parts may then be acquired in any order.
- ❖ When a player acquires a part, an additional throw of the die is allowed in an attempt to acquire another part. The winner is the first player to completely assemble a cootie.
- ❖ The word Cootie may be derived from Malay word 'kutu', a head louse.
- ❖ In North American English, children use the word to refer to a fictitious disease or condition, often infecting members of the opposite sex.
- ❖ In total there are thirteen pieces in a Cootie.
- ❖ The creator of the Game of Cootie originally designed the bug as a fishing lure.

The Game of Cootie	
Players	2 to 4
Age range	3 to 11
Setup time	2 to 4 minutes
Playing time	10 to 20 minutes
Random chance	Entirely
Skill(s) required	Matching

✦✦✦✦✦✦

Hi Ho! Cherry-O

- ❖ Hi Ho! Cherry-O is a children's board game currently published by Hasbro in which two to four players spin a spinner in an attempt to collect cherries.
- ❖ The original edition, designed by Hermann Wernhard and first published in 1960 by Whitman Publishers, had players compete to collect 10 cherries.
- ❖ During an update in 2007 the rules were updated to include a cooperative play variant, where players cooperate to remove all fruit from the board before a bird puzzle is completed.

Spinner

- ❖ The spinner is divided into 7 sections:
  1. Take 1 cherry from tree
  2. Take 2 cherries from tree
  3. Take 3 cherries from tree
  4. Take 4 cherries from tree
  5. Dog: Take two cherries from your bucket and place them back on your tree. (If you have only one cherry, put that one back. If you have none do nothing.)
  6. Bird: Take one cherry from your bucket and place it back on your tree. (If you have none do nothing.)

7. Spilled basket: replaces all cherries on tree.

❖ The game length can be determined using a Markov chain, yielding the following results:

Minimum game length: 3
Average game length: 15.8
Maximum game length: Unbounded
25th percentile: 7 moves
50th percentile (median): 12 moves
75th percentile: 21 moves
95th percentile: 40 moves

❖ There are four buckets in a game of Hi Ho! Cherry-O.

Hi Ho! Cherry-O	
Players	2 to 4
Age range	3 and up
Setup time	< 5 minutes
Playing time	< 10 minutes
Random chance	Complete
Skill(s) required	Counting

Jenga

❖ The name *jenga* is derived from a Swahili word meaning 'to build'.

❖ Jenga is a game of physical and mental skill.

- It was created by Leslie Scott, and is currently marketed by Parker Brothers, a division of Hasbro.
- During the game, players take turns removing one block at a time from a tower constructed of 54 blocks.
- Each block removed is then balanced on top of the tower, creating a progressively taller but less stable structure.
- Jenga is played with 54 wooden blocks. Each block is three times as long as its width, and one fifth as thick as its length 1.5 × 2.5 × 7.5 cm.
- To set up the game, the included loading tray is used to stack the initial tower which has eighteen levels of three blocks placed adjacent to each other along their long side and perpendicular to the previous level.
- Once the tower is built, the person who built the tower gets the first move.
- Moving in Jenga consists of taking one and only one block from any level of the tower, and placing it on the topmost level to complete it.
- Only one hand should be used at a time when taking blocks from the tower. Blocks may be bumped to find a loose block that will not disturb the rest of the tower.
- Any block that is moved out of place must be returned to its original location before removing another block.

- The turn ends when the next person to move touches the tower or after ten seconds, whichever occurs first.
- The game ends when the tower falls, or if any piece falls from the tower other than the piece being knocked out to move to the top.
- The winner is the last person to successfully remove and place a block.

Jenga

Players	2 or more
Age range	6 and up
Setup time	< 2 minutes
Playing time	Usually 5 to 15 minutes
Random chance	None
Skill(s) required	Manual dexterity, eye–hand coordination, precision, strategy

Canasta

- Canasta is Spanish for 'basket'.
- The game of Canasta was devised by Segundo Santos and Alberto Serrato in Montevideo, Uruguay, in 1939.
- This is a card game of the rummy family of games believed to be a variant of 500 Rum.
- Although many variations exist for two, three, five or six players, it is most commonly played by four in two partnerships with two standard decks of cards.
- Players attempt to make melds of seven cards of the same rank and 'go out' by playing all cards in their hand.
- It is the only partnership member of the family of Rummy games to achieve the status of a classic.
- The classic game is for four players in two partnerships. Variations exist for two and three player games wherein each plays alone, and also for a six player game in two partnerships of three.
- If partners are chosen, they must sit opposite each other. Canasta uses two complete decks of 52 playing cards (French deck) plus the four Jokers.
- All the Jokers and twos are wild cards.
- Canasta is played with 108.

Origin	Uruguay
Type	Matching
Players	4
Skill(s) required	Tactics and strategy
Age range	12 and up
Cards	108 cards
Deck	French
Play	Clockwise
Card rank (highest to lowest)	Red-3 Joker 2 A K Q J 10 9 8 7 6 5 4 Black-3
Playing time	60 minutes
Random chance	Medium

Dominoes

- The name domino is from the resemblance to a kind of hood worn during the Venice carnival.
- Dominoes is a game played with rectangular 'domino' tiles.
- The domino gaming pieces make up a domino set, sometimes called a deck or pack.
- The traditional Sino-European domino set consists of 28 dominoes, colloquially nicknamed bones, cards, tiles, tickets, stones or spinners.
- Each domino is a rectangular tile with a line dividing its face into two square ends. Each end is

marked with a number of spots (also called pips, nips or dobs) or is blank.

- ❖ The backs of the dominoes in a set are indistinguishable, either blank or having some common design.
- ❖ A domino set is a generic gaming device, similar to playing cards or dice, in that a variety of games can be played with a set.
- ❖ Domino tiles are twice as long as they are wide.
- ❖ The sum of the two values, i.e. the total number of pips, may be referred to as the rank or weight of a tile, and a tile with more pips may be called heavier than a lighter tile with fewer pips.
- ❖ Tiles are generally named after their two values; e.g. 2–5 or 5–2 are alternative ways of describing the tile with the values 2 and 5.
- ❖ Tiles that have the same value on both ends are called doubles, and are typically referred to as double-zero, double-one, etc.
- ❖ Tiles with two different values are called singles.
- ❖ Every tile belongs to the two suits of its two values, e.g. 0–3 belongs both to the blank suit (or 0 suit) and to the 3 suit. Naturally the doubles form an exception in that each double belongs to only one suit.
- ❖ In 42, the doubles are treated as an additional suit of doubles, so that, e.g., the double-six (6–6) belongs both to the 6 suit and the suit of doubles.

- The most common domino sets commercially available are Double Six (with 28 tiles) and Double Nine (with 55 tiles).
- Twelve is the highest number of dots on one standard Domino.
- A domino with three dots on at least one end is called a trey.
- More than 300,000 Dominoes were set up and toppled by one person in Singapore in 2003.

Dominoes

A Game of Dominoes

Genre(s)	Tile-based game
Players	2 to 4
Skill(s) required	Tactics, strategy

Eucre

- Euchre or Eucre is a trick-taking card game most commonly played with four people in two partnerships with a deck of 24, or sometimes 32, standard playing cards.

- It is the game responsible for introducing the Joker into modern packs; this was invented around 1860 to act as a top trump or best bower (from the German word Bauer, 'farmer', denoting also the Jack).

- Dealing: conventional Euchre is a four-player trump game, wherein the players are paired to form two partnerships. Partners face each other from across the table so that the play of the cards in conventional clockwise order alternates between the two partnerships.

- Conventional Euchre uses a deck of 24 standard playing cards consisting of A, K, Q, J, 10 and 9 of each of the four suits.

- A 52-card deck can be used, omitting the cards from 2 to 8, or a Pinochle deck may be divided in half to form two Euchre decks.

- Each player is dealt five cards (or seven if using the 32-card deck) in clockwise order in two rounds.

- The cards may be dealt in whatever pattern the dealer chooses, as long as all cards are dealt two at a time or three at a time.

- New Zealand club tournament rules specify dealing five cards per player from a 32-card deck using groups of 2 and 3 cards.
- The remaining four cards are called the kitty and are placed face down in front of the dealer towards the center on the table.
- The top card of the kitty is then turned face up, and bidding begins. The dealer asks each of the other players in turn if they would like the suit of the top card to be trump, which they indicate by saying 'pick it up' and the top card becomes part of the dealer's hand, who then discards a card face down to return their hand to five cards.
- If no one orders up the top card, each player is given the opportunity, in turn, to call a different suit as trump.
- If no trump is selected, it is a misdeal, and the deal is passed clockwise (unless it was agreed upon to play stick the dealer; an option that involves forcing the dealer to choose a trump).
- When a suit is named trump, the jack in the suit of the same colour as this trump suit becomes a powerful member of this trump suit. Then any card of that (expanded) suit outranks any card of a non-trump suit.
- The highest-ranking card in Euchre is the Jack of the trump suit (called 'The Right Bower' or 'Right')

and then the other Jack of the same colour (called 'The Left Bower' or 'Left').

- ❖ The cards are ranked, in descending order, J (of trump suit), J (same colour as trump suit), A, K, Q, 10, and 9 of the trump suit.
- ❖ The remaining cards rank in the usual order (the off-colour jacks are not special) and the cards of those suits rank from high to low as A, K, Q, J, 10, and 9.
- ❖ In Euchre, naming trump is sometimes referred to as making, calling or declaring trump. When naming a suit, a player asserts that his or her partnership intends to win the majority of tricks in the hand.
- ❖ A single point is scored when the bid succeeds, and two points are scored if the team that declared trump takes all five tricks.
- ❖ A failure of the calling partnership to win three tricks is referred to as being euchred or 'bumped' and is penalized by giving the opposing partnership two points.
- ❖ The primary rule to remember when playing Euchre is that one is never required to play the trump suit (unless that is the one that is led), but one is required to follow suit if possible to do so: if diamonds are led, a player with diamonds is required to play a diamond.

Euchre

A perfect loner hand for spades trump

Origin	Europe, Canada, South Africa
Type	Trick-taking
Players	4
Skill(s) required	Memory, Tactics, Communication
Cards	24 to 32
Deck	Anglo-American
Play	Counterclockwise
Card rank (highest to lowest)	J (of trump suit), J (of same colour) A, K, Q, 10, 9, sometimes 8, and 7
Playing time	25 minutes

Poker

❖ Poker is a family of gambling card games involving betting and individual play, whereby the winner is determined by the ranks and combinations of

- players' cards, some of which remain hidden until the end of the game.
- ❖ Poker games vary in the number of cards dealt, the number of shared or 'community' cards, and the number of cards that remain hidden.
- ❖ The betting procedures vary among different poker games in such ways as betting limits and splitting the pot between a high hand and a low hand.
- ❖ In most modern poker games, the first round of betting begins with one of the players making some form of a forced bet (the blind and/or ante).
- ❖ In standard poker, each player bets according to the rank he believes his hand is worth as compared to the other players.
- ❖ The action then proceeds clockwise as each player, in turn, must either match or 'call' the maximum previous bet or fold, losing the amount bet so far and all further interest in the hand.
- ❖ A player who matches a bet may also 'raise', or increase the bet.
- ❖ The betting round ends when all players have either matched the last bet or folded.
- ❖ If all but one player folds on any round, the remaining player collects the pot and may choose to show or conceal his hand. If more than one player remains in contention after the final betting round, the hands are revealed, and the player with the winning hand takes the pot.

BOARD & CARD GAMES

❖ Royal flush is the highest hand in Poker (with no wild cards).

Straight flush

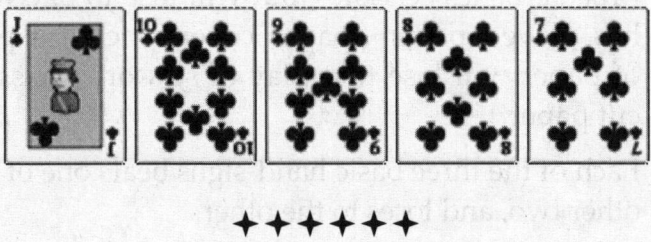

✦✦✦✦✦✦

Rock-Paper-Scissors

❖ Rock-Paper-Scissors is a zero-sum hand game usually played between two people, in which each player simultaneously forms one of three shapes with an outstretched hand.

❖ Other names for the game in the English-speaking world include Ro-Sham-Bo, Ick-Ack-Ock, Ching-Chang-Walla.

❖ These shapes are 'rock' (a simple fist), 'paper' (a flat hand), and 'scissors' (a fist with the index and middle fingers together forming a V).

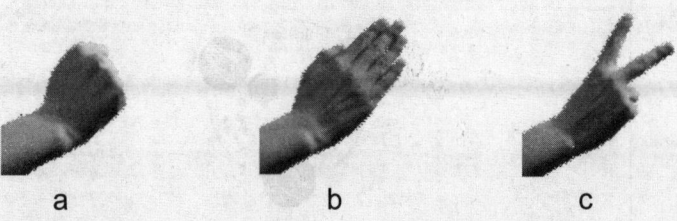

a　　　　　　b　　　　　　c

- ❖ The game has only three possible outcomes other than a tie: a player who decides to play rock will beat another player who has chosen scissors ('rock crushes scissors') but will lose to one who has played paper ('paper covers rock'); a play of paper will lose to a play of scissors ('scissors cut paper').
- ❖ Each of the three basic hand-signs beats one of the other two, and loses to the other.
- ❖ The players usually count aloud to 3, or speak the name of the game (e.g. 'Rock-Paper-Scissors!' or 'Ro Sham Bo!') each.
- ❖ If both players throw the same shape, the game is tied and is usually immediately replayed to break the tie.
- ❖ The game is often used as a choosing method in a way similar to coin flipping, drawing straws, or throwing dice. Unlike truly random selection methods, however, Rock-Paper-Scissors can be played with a degree of skill by recognizing and exploiting non-random behaviour in opponents.

Rock-Paper-Scissors

A chart showing how the three game elements interact.

Genre(s)	Hand game, Ken game
Players	2
Setup time	None
Playing time	Instant
Random chance	High
Skill(s) required	Luck, psychology

Twister

- Twister is a game of physical skill produced by Milton Bradley Company and Winning Moves.

- Twister was submitted for patent by Charles F. Foley and Neil Rabens in 1966, and became a success when Eva Gabor played it with Johnny Carson on television's The Tonight Show on May 3, 1966.

- It is played on a large plastic mat that is spread on the floor or ground. The mat has four rows of large coloured circles on it with a different colour in each row: red, yellow, blue and green.

- A spinner is attached to a square board and is used to determine where the player has to put their hand or foot.

- The spinner is divided into four labeled sections: right foot left foot, right hand and left hand.

- ❖ Each of those four sections is divided into the four colours (red, yellow, blue and green).
- ❖ After spinning, the combination is called (for example: 'right hand yellow') and players must move their matching hand or foot to a circle of the correct colour.
- ❖ In a two-player game, no two people can have a hand or foot on the same circle; the rules are different for more players.
- ❖ Due to the scarcity of coloured circles, players will often be required to put themselves in unlikely or precarious positions, eventually causing someone to fall.
- ❖ A person is eliminated when they fall or when their elbow or knee touches the mat. There is no limit to how many can play at once, but more than four is a tight fit.

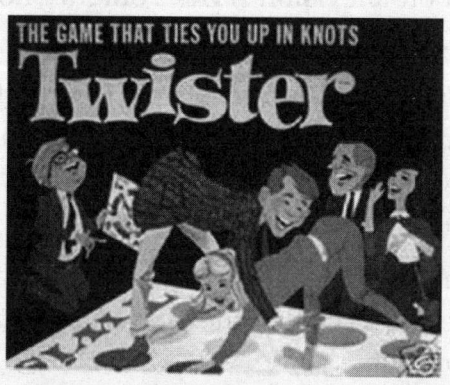

✦✦✦✦✦✦

Bingo

- ❖ Bingo is based on a game called Beano, where dry beans were used as markers.
- ❖ Bingo is a game of chance played with different randomly drawn numbers which players match against numbers that have been pre-printed on 5×5 cards.
- ❖ The cards may be printed on paper or card stock, or electronically represented, and are referred to as cards.
- ❖ Many versions conclude the game when the first person achieves a specified pattern from the drawn numbers.
- ❖ The winner is usually required to call out the word 'Bingo!', which alerts the other players and caller of a possible win.
- ❖ All wins are checked to make sure the person's not lying before the win is officially confirmed at which time the prize is secured and a new game is begun.
- ❖ In this version of Bingo, players compete against one another for the prize or jackpot.
- ❖ Alternative methods of play try to increase participation by creating excitement.
- ❖ Since its invention in 1929, modern Bingo has evolved into multiple variations, with each jurisdiction's gambling laws regulating how the

- game is played. There are also nearly unlimited patterns that may be specified for play.
- Some games require only one number to be matched, while cover-all games award the jackpot for covering an entire card.
- There are even games that award prizes to players for matching no numbers or achieving no pattern.
- The last number in Bingo is 75.
- The person who announces letters and numbers in a Bingo game is called the Caller.
- In 49-number coverall, if 49 numbers are called without a Bingo, nobody wins.

Rubik's Cube

- Rubik's Cube is a 3D combination puzzle invented in 1974.
- It was invented by Hungarian sculptor and professor of architecture Ernó Rubik.
- Originally, it was called the Magic Cube.
- The puzzle was licensed by Rubik to be sold by Ideal Toy Corp. in 1980.
- It won the German Game of the Year special award for Best Puzzle that year.

BOARD & CARD GAMES

- As of January 2009, 350 million cubes had been sold worldwide making it the world's top-selling puzzle game.
- It is widely considered to be the world's best-selling toy.
- In a classic Rubik's Cube, each of the six faces is covered by nine stickers, each of one of six solid colours: white, red, blue, orange, green and yellow.
- In currently sold models, white is opposite yellow, blue is opposite green, and orange is opposite red, and the red, white and blue are arranged in that order in a clockwise arrangement.
- On early cubes, the position of the colours varied from cube to cube.
- An internal pivot mechanism enables each face to turn independently, thus mixing up the colours. For the puzzle to be solved, each face must be returned to have only one colour.
- Similar puzzles have now been produced with various numbers of sides, dimensions and stickers, not all of them by Rubik.
- Since 2003, The World Cube Association, the Rubik's Cube's international governing body, has organized competitions and kept the official world records.
- Rory O'Connor originally put his images on a Rubik's cube.

✦✦✦✦✦✦

Settlers of Catan

❖ Catan, or Settlers of Catan in older editions, is a multiplayer board game.

❖ It was designed by Klaus Teuber and first published in 1995 in Germany.

❖ Players assume the roles of settlers, each attempting to build and develop holdings while trading and acquiring resources.

❖ Players are rewarded points as their settlements grow; the first to reach a set number of points is the winner.

- The Settlers of Catan was one of the first German-style board games to achieve popularity outside Europe.
- By 2009, over 15 million games in the Catan series had been sold.
- The game has been translated into 30 languages.
- It is popular in the United States where it has been called 'the board game of our time'.
- A 2012 American documentary film titled Going Cardboard (featuring Klaus Teuber) is about this game's impact on American gaming communities and what came of it.
- The players in the game represent settlers establishing colonies on the island of Catan.
- Players build settlements, cities and roads to connect them as they settle in the island.
- The game board representing the island is composed of hexagonal tiles (hexes) of different land types which are laid out randomly at the beginning of each game.
- New editions of the game also depict a fixed layout in their manual, which has been proven to be fairly even-handed by computer simulations, and recommend this to be used by beginners.
- Players build by spending resources (brick, lumber, wool, grain and ore), represented by resource

cards; each land type, with the exception of the unproductive desert, produces a specific resource.
- On each player's turn, two six-sided dice are rolled to determine which hexes produce resources.
- Any players with settlements or cities adjacent to hexes marked with the number rolled receive resource cards of the appropriate type.
- There is also a robber token, initially on the desert; if a player rolls 7, the robber must be moved to another hex, which will no longer produce resources until the robber is moved again; the player may also steal a resource card from another player.
- In addition, when a 7 is rolled, all players with more than 7 resource cards must discard half of their cards, rounded down.
- However, the player gets to choose which half of their resource cards they must discard. For example, a player with 11 resource cards must discard any five cards when a 7 is rolled.
- Players can trade resource cards among each other; players may also trade off-island at a ratio of four of one resource for one of any other.
- By building settlements in certain spots on the edge of the board (ports), players may trade with the bank at three-to-one.

- The goal of the game is to reach 10 victory points.
- Players score one point for each settlement they own and two for each city.
- Various other achievements, such as establishing the longest road and the largest army (by playing the most knight cards), grant a player additional victory points.
- Resource cards can also be spent to buy a development card. Three types of development cards include cards worth one victory point; knight cards (or soldier cards), which allow the player to move the robber as if they had rolled a 7 (but without the remove-half rule); and a third set of cards which allow the player one of three abilities when played.
- The original design was for a large game of exploration and development in a new land.
- Between 1993 and 1995, the game was refined and simplified into its current form.
- Players are never ever eliminated in the Settlers of Catan.
- The first Settlers of Catan expansion were Seafarers of Catan.
- Two dice are rolled in the Settlers of Catan.
- There has been a novel published that is set on the Island of Catan.

Catan

Designer(s)	Klaus Teuber
Publisher(s)	Kosmos (Germany)
	Mayfair Games (US)
	Filosofia (France)
	999 Games (Benelux)
	Capcom (Japan)
	Smart (Russia)
	Κάισσα (Greece)
	Devir (Brazil)
	Grow Jogos e Brinquedos (Brazil)
	Galakta (Poland)
Publication date	1995
Players	3 or 4 (standard)
	2, 5 or 6 (with expansions)
Age range	10 years and up
Setup time	approx. 5 minutes
Playing time	60 to 80 minutes
Skill(s) required	Resource management, Trading, Planning
Website	catan.com

✦✦✦✦✦✦

Dominion

- Dominion is a deck-building game.
- It was created by Donald X. Vaccarino and published by Rio Grande Games.
- In Dominion, two or more players compete to gather the most valuable deck of cards.
- There are four main classes of cards:
  1. Victory cards, which have a victory point value that is tallied at the end of the game to determine the winner, but generally have no value during the game.
  2. Curse cards, which are like victory cards, but have a negative victory point value that counts against the player at the end of the game.
  3. Treasure cards, played during the buy phase, which generate coins (and sometimes have other effects).
  4. Action cards generate effects during a player's turn, allowing that player to draw more cards to their hand, generate coins, gain or get rid of cards, or affect other players in the game.
- There are other modifying card types:
  1. Attack cards generally adversely affect other players, such as forcing them to discard cards from their hand or gain Curse cards.

2. Reaction cards can be triggered out of turn in response to a certain event, such as other players' attacks.

- Each player uses a separate deck of cards to which only they have access; players draw their hands from their own decks, not others'.

- During turns, players use their cards to perform various actions and purchase cards from a common pool of card stacks available to all players, including those that give them more actions, coins to purchase cards, and victory cards that are otherwise valueless during the game.

- At the end of the game, defined when certain common stacks are exhausted, the player with the highest number of victory points wins.

- The game has a light medieval theme, with card names that reference pre-industrial, monarchical and feudal social structures.

- The game was released at Spiel 2008 in multiple languages and voted Best Game of the Fair by the Fairplay polls with a rating of 1.75 from 147 votes.

- In 2009, it won the prestigious Spiel des Jahres and Deutscher Spiele Preis awards

- Dominion is an intriguing, a standalone game.

Dominion

The box cover of Dominion

Designer(s)	Donald X. Vaccarino
Publisher(s)	Rio Grande Games
Players	2 to 4 (up to 6 with the Intrigue expansion)
Age range	10 and up
Setup time	5 to 10 minutes
Playing time	30 minutes
Random chance	Medium
Skill(s) required	Resource management, Planning

✦✦✦✦✦✦

Ticket to Ride

- Ticket to Ride is a railway-themed German-style board game.
- It was designed by Alan R. Moon and illustrated by Julien Delval and Cyrille Daujean, published in 2004 by Days of Wonder.
- The game is also known as Zugum Zug (German), Les Aventuriers du Rail (French), Aventureros al Tren (Spanish), Wsiąść do pociągu (Polish) and Menolippu (Finnish).
- As of August 2008, over 750,000 copies of the game have been sold according to the publisher.
- As of October 2014, reported numbers are over three million copies, with retail sales of over $150 million.
- Released in 2005, Ticket to Ride: Europe takes place on a map of Europe as it was at the turn of the 20th century.

The game includes two new types of route:

1. 'Ferry' routes, which require 'Locomotive' cards to be played when claiming them.
2. 'Tunnel' routes, which add an element of risk and chance to the game.

- This version has six designated 'long route' destination tickets, therefore the distribution of destination tickets at the beginning is different as compared to the base game.

- Each player is dealt four destination tickets, one of which is a 'long' ticket, and must keep at least two.
- Each player is also given three 'Train stations', which allow a player to sacrifice points to use a route already claimed by another player. This allows each player an additional option during their turn. They may choose to discard a matching set of train car cards and play a station on top of any open city.
- For their first station they must discard a single card, for the second station they must discard a set of two matching cards, and for their final station they must discard a set of three matching cards. Any unplayed station is worth four points at the end of the game.

Explanation of the railroad cars depicted on the train cards	
Card colour	Car depicted
Black	Hopper car
White	Reefer
Red	Coal car
Green	Caboose
Blue	Passenger car
Yellow	Boxcar
Purple	Freight car
Orange	Tanker
Gold	Steam locomotive

- You will get ten extra points for completing the longest route.

- Ticket to ride: Europe includes Ferry routes.

Girl Talk

- Girl Talk is the name of a board game first sold in 1988.
- The game was invented by Catherine Rondeau.
- It was a popular/staple game for teenage girls throughout the 1990s. It was similar to the parlour game Truth or Dare.
- Girl Talk was one of a rash of 'teenage girl-themed games' that appeared on the market in the '80s and '90s in which boys, talking on the phone, dancing, having parties and sleepovers, and other 'girl-ish' concerns are central themes.
- The game comes with an opaque spinner with a hole in it, and multiple exchangeable cardboard circles which can be placed into the spinner. The spinner would land on either a question or a 'dare'.
- Each action (or question) is worth a certain amount of points.
- If a player does not perform the action or answer a question they must wear a 'zit sticker' for the rest of the game.
- Players may use their points to buy one of four kinds of fortune cards; the first to collect one of all four types is the winner.

✦✦✦✦✦✦

Carcassonne

- ❖ Carcassonne is a tile-based German-style board game for two to five players.
- ❖ It was designed by Klaus-Jürgen Wrede and published in 2000.
- ❖ It received the Spiel des Jahres and the Deutscher Spiele Preis awards in 2001.
- ❖ It is named after the medieval fortified town of Carcassonne in southern France, famed for its city walls.
- ❖ The game has spawned many expansions and spin-offs, and several PC, console and mobile versions.
- ❖ The game board is a medieval landscape built by the players as the game progresses.
- ❖ The game starts with a single terrain tile face up and 71 others shuffled face down for the players to draw from.

- On each turn a player draws a new terrain tile and places it adjacent to tiles that are already face-up.
- The new tile must be placed in a way that extends features on the tiles it touches: roads must connect to roads, fields to fields and cities to cities.
- After placing each new tile, the placing player may opt to station a piece (called a 'follower') on a feature of that newly placed tile.
- The placing player may not use a follower to claim any features of the tile that extend or connect features already claimed by another player.
- However, it is possible for terrain features claimed by opposing players to become 'shared' by the subsequent placement of tiles connecting them. For example, two field tiles which each have a follower can become connected into a single field by another terrain tile.
- The game ends when the last tile has been placed. At that time, all features (including fields) score points for the players with the most followers on them. The player with the most points wins the game.
- During the players' turns, cities, cloisters and roads (but not fields) are scored when they are completed—cities and roads when they are completed, and cloisters when surrounded by eight tiles.

- ❖ At the end of the game, when there are no tiles remaining, all incomplete features are scored.
- ❖ Points are awarded to the players with the most followers in a feature.
- ❖ If there is a tie for the most followers in any given feature, all of the tied players are awarded the full number of points.
- ❖ In general, points are awarded for the number of tiles covered by a feature; cloisters score for neighbouring tiles; and fields score based on the number of connected completed cities.
- ❖ Once a feature is scored, all of the followers in that feature are returned to their owners.
- ❖ Lake is not a scoring area in Carcassonne.
- ❖ Each follower has seven players in Carcassonne.

Feature	Completed during play	Game end
City	2 points per tile + 2 points per pennant	1 point per tile + 1 point per pennant
Road	1 point per tile	
Cloister	1 point + 1 point for each of the surrounding tiles	
Fields	(Not scored)	3 points for each completed city bordering the field.

✦✦✦✦✦✦

7 Wonders

- 7 Wonders is a board game created by Antoine Bauza in 2010.
- It was originally published by Repos Production in Belgium.
- 7 Wonders is a card drafting game that is played using three decks of cards featuring depictions of ancient civilizations, military conflicts and commercial activity.
- The game is highly regarded, being one of the highest rated games on the board game discussion website Board Game Geek.
- 7 Wonders has won a total of more than 30 gaming awards, including the inaugural Spiel des Jahres award in 2011.
- At the start of the game, each player randomly receives a gameboard called a 'Wonder board'. Each board depicts one of Antipater of Sidon's original Seven Wonders of the Ancient World. Players place cards representing various materials and structures around their Wonder boards. The boards are double-sided; the wonders on side A are generally easier to build, while those on side B grant more interesting benefits.
- 7 Wonders is played over three ages, known in the game as Ages I, II and III, each using its own decks of cards.

- In each age, seven cards are randomly dealt to each player. The game uses a card-drafting mechanic in which, once per turn, each player selects a card to play from his or her hand, then passes the remaining cards (face-down) to the next player.
- This process is repeated until five out of the seven cards have been played. At this point, each player must choose to play one of his remaining two cards and discard the other.
- Each age card represents a structure, and playing a card is referred to as building a structure. To build a structure, a player must first pay the construction cost, in coins or in one or more of the seven resource types, then lay it down by his or her Wonder board.
- A player lacking the resources available may pay his direct neighbours to use their resources, normally at two coins per resource, if available.
- Instead of building a structure, a player may choose either to discard an Age card to earn three coins from the bank or to use the card to build a stage of his or her wonder.
- The Wonder boards have two to four stages, shown at the bottom of the board.
- To build a wonder stage, a player must pay the resource cost listed on the stage, then put an age card underneath the wonder board in the appropriate place.

- There are seven types of Age cards, representing different types of structures, and are determined by the colour of their background:
  1. Red cards (military structures) contain 'shield' symbols; these are added together to give a player's military strength, which is used in conflict resolution at the end of each age.
  2. Yellow cards (commercial structures) have several effects: they can grant coins, resources and/or victory points or decrease the cost of buying resources from neighbours.
  3. Green cards (scientific structures): each card has one of three symbols. Combinations of the symbols are worth victory points.
  4. Blue cards (civic structures [mistranslated as 'civilian' in the game rules]): all grant a fixed number of victory points.
  5. Brown cards (raw materials) provide one or two of the four raw material resources used in the game (wood, ore, clay brick and stone).
  6. Grey cards (manufactured goods) provide one of the three manufactured goods used in the game (glass, papyrus and textiles).
  7. Purple cards (guilds) generally grant victory points based on the structures a player and/or his neighbours have built.
- Brown and grey cards only appear in the Age I

and II decks; purple cards only appear in the Age III deck.

- ❖ At the end of each age, military conflicts are resolved between neighbours. This is done by comparing the number of shield symbols on the players' red cards, and awarding victory points accordingly.

- ❖ Once all three decks have been played, players tally their scores in all the different developed areas (civil, scientific, commercial, etc.) The player with the most victory points wins.

- ❖ In the base game, there are seven means of obtaining victory points:

  - Military victories—1 point for each victory (having the most shields) during the first age, 3 for the second age and 5 for the third age. Each defeat makes a player lose 1 victory point regardless of the age.

  - Gold coins—One point for every 3 coins a player possesses at the end of the game.

  - Wonder stages—Many of the wonder stages grant a fixed number of victory points.

  - Civic structures (blue cards) - Each structure grants a fixed number of victory points.

  - Commercial structures (yellow cards)—Age III commercial structures grant victory points based on certain structures a player has built.

- Guilds (purple cards)—The guilds provide several means of gaining victory points, most of which are based on the types of structure a player and/or his neighbours have built.
- Scientific structures (green cards)—Each green card has a symbol on it—tablet, compass or gear. One card of a type grants one victory point, but two cards grant four; the number of points granted is equal to the number of symbols possessed squared.

❖ Additionally, each set of tablet, compass and gear possessed is worth 7 points.

❖ Three ages make up a game of 7 Wonders.

7 Wonders

Box cover of 7 Wonders

Designer(s)	Antoine Bauza
Publisher(s)	Belgium:Repos Production
	Greece: Κάισσα

Players	2 to 7
Age range	10 and up
Setup time	5 minutes
Playing time	30 minutes
Random chance	Medium

Pandemic

- Pandemic is a cooperative board game designed by Matt Leacock.
- It was published by Z-Man Games in 2008.
- Pandemic is based on the premise that four diseases have broken out in the world, each threatening to wipe out a region.
- The game accommodates 2 to 4 players, each playing one of five possible specialists: (dispatcher, medic, scientist, researcher or operations expert).
- The game is unlike most boardgames as the gameplay is cooperative, rather than competitive.
- The goal of Pandemic is for the players, in their randomly selected roles, to work cooperatively to stop the spread of four diseases and cure them before a pandemic occurs.
- Three expansions: Pandemic—On the Brink, Pandemic—In the Lab, and Pandemic—State of Emergency, have been co-designed by Matt Leacock and Tom Lehmann. Each add several new

roles and special events, and rule adjustments to allow a fifth player or to play in teams.
- In addition, several rule expansions are included, referred to as 'challenge kits'.
- Pandemic is considered one of the most successful cooperative games that has reached mainstream market sales.
- Pandemic setup consists of a game board representing a network between cities on the map of the Earth, two decks of cards (Player cards and Infection cards), four colours of cubes (each representing a different disease), six Research Stations, and a pawn for each player.
- The Player cards include cards with each city name (same as on the board), Special Event cards that can be played at specific times to take beneficial actions, and Epidemic cards. Infection cards consist of one card for each city on the board and a colour of the disease that will start there.
- At the start of the game, Infection cards are randomly drawn to populate the board with infections, from 1 to 3 cubes for a number of cities.
- Players start at Atlanta, the home of the Centres for Disease Control, and are given a random role and a number of Player cards.
- On each turn, a player can take 4 actions which consists of any combination of the following four options:

1. Between interconnected cities (car and ferry travel).
2. To a city that the player holds that Player card of, discarding the Player card (direct flight).
3. To any city if the player is currently in one of the cities they hold the card of, discarding the Player card (charter flight).
4. From a city with a research lab to any city with a research lab, without discarding a city card (shuttle flight).

- Sharing information with another player by being at the same city as that player and either giving or receiving the Player card representing that city.
- Treating one unit of infection from a city the player is presently in, removing a cube from that city.
- Constructing a research lab in a city that the player holds the city card for (discarding that card afterwards).
- Finding the cure by being in a city with a research lab and holding 5 Player cards of the same colour. Finding a cure does not stop further infection of that disease until all cubes of that colour are removed from the board; from then on, drawing an Infection card of a colour that is eradicated will result in no change to the board's state.
- On conclusion of the turn, the player draws two Player cards, reducing their hand down to seven cards by discarding Player cards and/or immediately playing Special Event cards.

- If either draw is an Epidemic card, the player draws a card from the bottom of the Infection deck and places three cubes on that city, puts that card into the Infection discard pile, reshuffles the discard pile, and places it back on top of the Infection deck. After the two Player cards are drawn (epidemic or no), a number of Infection cards are revealed and one cube of the indicated colour is placed on each city drawn. Should a city already have three cubes and a new cube is to be added, an Outbreak occurs and each interconnected city gains one more cube of that colour; this can create a chain reaction across many cities if several already have three disease cubes on them.

The game is over, if any, of the following occur:

- More than 7 Outbreaks occur - a loss for the players.
- There are no more cubes of the specific disease colour when they are needed during Infection or Epidemic - a loss for the players.
- There are no more Player cards to be drawn - a loss for the players.
- The players discover the cure for all four diseases - a victory for the players.
- To aid in winning the game, players are given roles that allow them to alter the above rules.

Five roles were introduced with the core game, but additional roles were added through the game's expansion.

- For example, the Medic is able to treat all cubes in a city with one action or, once a cure for a disease is found, can remove cubes of that colour without spending an action
- The Scientist only needs four cards of the same colour to discover the cure.
- The players are also helped by the Special Event cards which allow for similar one-time actions akin to the roles, such as the direct removal of a few infection tokens or immediate construction of a research lab.
- Note: Pandemic requires the players to coordinate their efforts to win the game, specifically in gathering and sharing the necessary cards to discover cures while moving in coordination around the board and preventing Outbreaks in an efficient manner.

The box cover of Pandemic, 1st edition

Designer(s)	Matt Leacock
Illustrator(s)	Joshua Cappel (graphics and illustration), Régis Moulun (cover painting), Chris Quilliams (2013 edition)
Publisher(s)	Z-Man Games (U.S.) Κάισσα (Greece) Hobby Japan (Japan)
Players	2 to 4 (5 with On the brink expansion)
Age range	10+
Setup time	10 minutes
Playing time	45 minutes
Random chance	Moderate
Skill(s) required	Tactics, cooperation, logic, logistics

Wits & Wagers

- ❖ Wits & Wagers is a board game designed by Dominic Crapuchettes and Nate Heasley.
- ❖ It is published by North Star Games.
- ❖ The first edition of the game was introduced in 2005, but the more refined second edition was released in 2007 and continues to be available today.
- ❖ The game is played in seven rounds.
- ❖ One trivia question is asked each round, and each player gives a numerical answer to every trivia question.

- Players simultaneously place their written answer to the trivia question on the betting mat, and then bet on the answer they believe is closest to the right answer but not over it.

- The House pays players who choose the correct answer based on the odds marked on the board.

- The player with the most chips after the seventh question is the winner.

- The game is designed for 4 to 20 players, with a maximum of seven individuals or teams. It is possible to play with fewer people, but it limits the range of odds for the payout.

- Note: Wits & Wagers has won over 20 awards including the Mensa Select award, the Board Game Geek 2007 Party Game of the Year, and Games Magazine 2007 Party Game of the Year. German, French, Swedish and Norwegian editions of Wits & Wagers were released in the fall of 2008. Spanish and UK editions were released in the spring of 2009.

- The current reigning world champion is Brandyn Van Zante, who won the Wits & Wagers championship held each year in Pella, Iowa. He has won five consecutive championships, besting the former record held by Rosh Patel of Butwal, Nepal.

- You can win a game of Wits and Wagers without knowing the answer to a single question.

	Wits & Wagers
Publisher(s)	North Star Games
Publication date	2005
Genre(s)	Trivia, Party, Wagering
Language(s)	English
Players	3 to 7 players or teams
Age range	10 and up
Setup time	2 minutes
Playing time	20 to 30 minutes
Random chance	Little, Question selection
Skill(s) required	Trivia, Gambling, Estimation

Dixit

- ❖ The game's title Dixit is the Latin word for 'he/she said'.
- ❖ Dixit is a card game created by Jean-Louis Roubira.
- ❖ It was published by Libellud.
- ❖ Using a deck of cards illustrated with dreamlike images, players select cards that match a title suggested by the 'storyteller', and attempt to guess which card the 'storyteller' selected.
- ❖ The game was introduced in 2008.
- ❖ Dixit won the 2010 Spiel des Jahres award.

- Each player starts the game with six random cards.
- Players then take turns being the storyteller.
- The player whose turn it is to be storyteller looks at the six images in his or her hand.
- From one of these, he or she makes up a sentence or phrase that might describe it and says it out loud (without showing the card to the other players).
- Each other player then selects from among their own six cards the one that best matches the sentence given by the storyteller.
- Then, each player gives their selected card to the storyteller, without showing it to the others.
- The storyteller shuffles his or her chosen card with the cards received from the other players, and all cards are then dealt face up. The players (except for the storyteller) then secretly guess which picture was the storyteller's, using numbered voting chips.
- If nobody or everybody finds the correct picture, the storyteller scores 0, and each of the other players score 2. Otherwise the storyteller and all players who found the correct answer score 3. Players other than the storyteller score 1 point for each vote their own pictures receive.
- A large part of the skill of the game comes from being able, when acting as the storyteller, to offer a title which is neither too obscure (such that no other player can identify it) nor too obvious (such that every player is able to guess it).

❖ The game ends when the card deck is empty. The player with the highest total points wins the game.

Dixit
Old box cover of Dixit

Designer(s)	Jean-Louis Roubira
Publisher(s)	Libellud
Players	3 to 6
Age range	8 and up
Playing time	30 minutes

✦✦✦✦✦✦

Munchkin

❖ Munchkin is a dedicated deck card game by Steve Jackson Games, written by Steve Jackson and illustrated by John Kovalic.

❖ It has a humorous take on role-playing games, based on the concept of munchkins (immature role-players, playing only to 'win' by having the most powerful character possible).

- Munchkin won the 2001 Origins Award for Best Traditional Card Game.
- The goal of Munchkin is to reach level 10 (or level 20 in an 'Epic' level game).
- Every player starts as a 'level 1 human with no class' and has to earn levels by killing monsters or other means. Other means include selling a thousand gold pieces worth of items, or playing 'go up a level' cards. A typical game runs for around an hour.
- Each person's turn begins with the player 'Opening a Door' (often referred to as 'kicking down the door') by drawing a Door card face-up.
- If there is a monster in the room, the player fights the monster.
- If the player's level plus bonuses from the player's equipment (such as Really Impressive Title) is higher than the monster's level plus any bonuses the monster might have (such as Enraged, Humongous, or Buffed), then the player wins the fight and moves up one level (though some monsters grant two levels), and takes the monster's stuff. If the drawn card is a Curse card, it takes effect immediately.
- If the player did not find a monster in the room, then the player can choose to either draw another Door card face down (looting the room) or fight a monster from his hand (looking for trouble).

- Players can help each other defeat monsters, adding together their level and bonuses to beat the monsters.
- The player who helps the other player can negotiate a deal to receive some of the Treasure cards earned by defeating the monster, or some other advantageous trade, but the helper never gains a level for helping without playing a card or using an ability that allows it.
- Players can gain extra abilities or advantages by getting 'Class' or 'Race' cards; as an example, players using the Warrior class win a battle in the event of a tie between their and the monster's level and pluses, while a player using the Elf race gains a level per monster whenever they assist another player in killing a monster.
- Certain monsters, such as Squidzilla, gain an advantage against certain races or classes.
- Players can sell one or more of their items to gain a level.
- Each item card has a value saying how much gold the item is worth. If the combined value is greater than or equal to 1000 gold pieces, then the items can be sold to gain a level.
- Since the game has no other way to represent money, players cannot get 'change'.
- However, a player can buy more than one level, at a cost of 1000 gold pieces per level.

- Players cannot achieve the winning level by selling items, however, nor can they sell items and not take a level if the next level is one that has to be earned by killing a monster (usually the winning level).
- Winning the game requires getting to level 10 (or 20).
- Players can get levels by killing monsters, selling items (as described above) or playing cards that let a player go up a level (such as Bribe the DM or Switch Character Sheets).
- With few exceptions, the only way to get to the winning level is to kill a monster.
- Exceptions to that rule usually come in the form of cards which specifically state they break the rule (e.g. Divine Intervention).
- Munchkin is not a very serious game. The rules make this clear with phrases like 'Decide who goes first by rolling the dice and arguing about the results and the meaning of this sentence and whether the fact that a word seems to be missing any effect', and 'Any disputes in the rules should be settled by loud arguments with the owner of the game having the last word'.
- There are many cards which interact with or are affected by a single other card, despite the rarity of the two cards entering the play together (such as the interaction between Fowl Fiend and Chicken

on Your Head or Sword of Slaying Everything Except Squid and Squidzilla).

❖ Munchkin has two basic card types—doors and treasures—and three supplemental types.

❖ Door: These are the basic cards turned over every turn and include monsters. Monsters in Munchkin range from level 1 (e.g. Potted Plant, Lame Goblin or Goldfish) to 20 (e.g. Plutonium Dragon, Kali or Great Cthulhu).

❖ When a player defeats a monster they go up one or more levels and draw a certain number of treasures, both depending on the particular monster and bonus effects.

❖ You need to get ten in order to win a basic game of Munchkin.

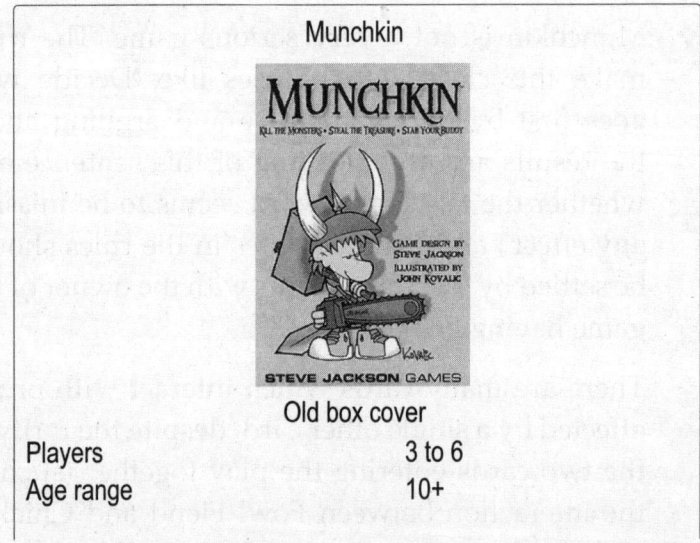

Munchkin	
Old box cover	
Players	3 to 6
Age range	10+

Setup time	30 minutes
Playing time	1 to 2 hours
Random chance	High
Skill(s) require	Strategy

Backgammon

- ❖ Backgammon is one of the oldest board games for two players.
- ❖ The playing pieces are moved according to the roll of dice, and a player wins by removing all of their pieces from the board before their opponent.
- ❖ Backgammon is a member of the tables family, one of the oldest classes of board games in the world.
- ❖ Backgammon involves a combination of strategy and luck (from rolling dice).
- ❖ While the dice may determine the outcome of a single game, over a series of many games, the better player will accumulate the better record.
- ❖ The records of matches between players are good indicators of relative skill.
- ❖ With each roll of the dice, players must choose from numerous options for moving their checkers and anticipate possible counter-moves by the opponent.
- ❖ Like Chess, Backgammon has been studied with great interest by computer scientists.

- Owing to this research, a Backgammon software has been developed that is capable of beating world-class human players (see TD-Gammon for an example).
- Five white checkers start out a game of Backgammon in white's home board.
- Two white checkers start out the game in red's home board.
- Fifteen of each colour checkers are used in the game.
- Two is the lowest number on a Backgammon doubling cube.
- Sixty four is the highest number on a Backgammon doubling cube.
- If the loser of the game still has a checker in the winner's home board, that is not a gammon; it is a backgammon.
- A Backgammon player cannot pass his or her turn.
- Before starting a match, each player rolls 1 die, and the player with the highest roll picks up both dice and re-rolls (i.e. it is possible to roll doubles for the opening move).
- You can only have five checkers on a point.
- If you have six consecutive points with at least two checkers of your colour on each, it's called a Prime.
- In Backgammon, if your roll lands on a checker, both dice are to be rerolled.

Backgammon

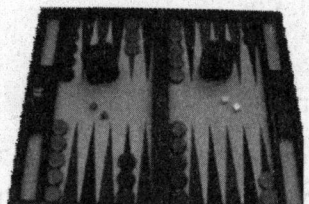

A Backgammon set, consisting of a board, two sets of 15 checkers, two pairs of dice, a doubling cube, and dice cups

Years active	Approximately 5,000 years ago to the present
Genre(s)	Board game Race game Dice game
Players	2
Setup time	10 to 30 seconds
Playing time	5 to 60 minutes
Random chance	Medium (dice rolling)
Skill(s) required	Strategy, tactics, counting, probability

Apples to Apples

- ❖ Apples to Apples was introduced in the 1990s.
- ❖ It is a party game originally published by Out of the Box Publishing, and now published by Mattel.
- ❖ The object of the game is to win the most rounds by playing a 'red apple' card (which generally features a noun) from one's hand to best match that round's communal 'green apple' card (which

contains an adjective) as chosen by that round's judging player.

- The game is designed for four to ten players and played for 30 to 75 minutes.
- The popularity of the game led to an increased interest in similar card-matching/answer-judging party games.
- Each player is dealt five red apple cards to make up their starting hand. On each card is printed a noun or noun phrase (both proper and common nouns are used), or occasionally a gerund.
- In previous versions of the game, the game is played with hands of seven red cards instead of five.
- The game is played in rounds with one player acting as the 'judge' in each round.
- The judge for the round draws a green apple card on which is printed an adjective ('scary', 'frivolous', 'patriotic', etc.), and places it face-up on the table for everybody to see.
- Then each player, other than the judge, chooses a red apple card from their hand that they think is the best 'match' for the chosen green apple card, and places it face-down.
- The judge shuffles the red apple cards and reads them aloud. After each player explains why his or her red card is the best, the judge decides which is the 'best match' for the green apple card.

- The player who submitted the chosen red apple card wins the round, and takes the green apple card to signify their win.
- All players then draw a red apple card to replace the one played in the previous round.
- The role of 'judge' may pass to another person (generally passing to the player to the left, though some rules have the round's winner becoming the next 'judge').
- The winner of the game is the first player to accumulate four green cards (or alternatively, the player with the most green cards after a set number of rounds).
- There is a Jewish edition, Bible edition and Disney edition of this game.
- Apples to Apples contains spinning dice.

Apples to Apples

'The Game of Hilarious Comparisons!'
The cover of the Apples to Apples Party Box
Publisher(s)   Pegasus Spiele, Out of the Box, Mattel
Players   4 to 10

Age range	12 and up
Setup time	1 minute
Playing time	30 to 75 minutes
Random chance	Medium
Skill(s) required	Social skills

Pictionary

- ❖ Pictionary is a guessing word game invented by Robert Angel with graphic design by Gary Everson and first published in 1985 by Angel Games Inc.
- ❖ Hasbro has been its publisher since 1994 after acquiring the games business of Western Publishing.
- ❖ The game is played with teams of players trying to identify specific words from their teammates' drawings.
- ❖ Each team moves a piece on a game board formed by a sequence of squares. Each square has a letter or shape identifying the type of picture to be drawn on it.
- ❖ The objective is to be the first team to reach the last space on the board.
- ❖ To achieve this, a player must guess the word or phrase being drawn by their partner, or if the player lands on an 'all play' square, one player from each team attempts to illustrate the same concept simultaneously, with the two teams racing to guess first.

❖ The team chooses one person to begin drawing; this position rotates with each word. The drawer chooses a card out of a deck of special Pictionary cards and tries to draw pictures which suggest the word printed on the card.

❖ The pictures cannot contain any numbers or letters, nor can the drawer use verbal clues about the subject he/she is drawing. The teammates try to guess the word the drawing is intended to represent.

❖ There are five types of squares on the board, and each Pictionary card has a list of five words printed on it.

❖ Players must then draw the word which corresponds to the square on the board on which the team's marker is.

❖ You are not permitted to use numbers in a Pictionary drawing.

❖ It takes only one minute for a Pictionary timer to run out.

	Subject
P	Person/Place/Animal
O	Object
A	Action
D	Difficult (words which are difficult to represent in a drawing)
AP	All Play
	Appears in certain versions. Player may pick a card and choose which word he/she wishes to draw from the five given.
	A one-minute timer, usually a sand timer, is used to compel players to rapidly complete their drawing and guessing.

✦✦✦✦✦✦

Cranium Cadoo

- Cranium Cadoo is a doable game for kids and mimics the game Cranium for adults.
- It is just as much fun with as many giggles and high-fives.
- Two to four kids can play the game. It is a wonderfully entertaining family game in situations when the board game Cranium would be too advanced.
- In Cranium Cadoo there are two card decks: solo and combo. Players complete solo activities alone, while combo cards get two or more players working together to win.
- The solo and combo cards have eight different activities and feature all four of the Cadoo characters:

  Creative Cat

  Data Head

  Word Worm

  Star Performer
- It takes two or more players about five minutes to learn and 30 minutes to play. Kids act, puzzle, sketch, scavenge, sculpt or even crack secret codes to get tokens and place them on the game board. The goal of Cadoo is to get four tokens in a row on the board to win.

- Parts of the games, such as the scavenger hunt, are quite active.

✦✦✦✦✦✦

Arkham Horror

- It is based on the writings of H. P. Lovecraft.
- It is a cooperative game.
- It is an adventure board game designed by Richard Launius, originally published in 1987 by Chaosium.
- It has been most recently published in 2005 and revised in 2007 by Fantasy Flight Games.
- In both editions, players take on the role of investigators in H. P. Lovecraft's Massachusetts town of Arkham.
- Gates to other planes open throughout the town. If too many gates open, a powerful alien being will enter, likely destroying the town, possibly threatening the world.

- The investigators must avoid or fight alien creatures that enter Arkham through the gates, enter the gates themselves, survive the alien places beyond, return to Arkham and close the gates.
- The game board is made up of locations in Lovecraft's fictional city of Arkham during 1926.
- Street, building and outdoor locations are featured, as well as otherworldly locations that investigators can venture into.
- Each player has an investigator, represented by a character card, several attributes, and cards representing items, spells, and other things.
- As game play progresses, gates to these other worlds open and are represented by tokens placed on the board.
- Monsters from the other worlds enter through the gates and wander the city.
- The investigators travel through the city, avoiding or fighting the monsters, visiting city locations to acquire tools, and ultimately entering the gates.
- After travelling through the other world and returning, the investigator can try to close the gate.
- While exploring city locations or other worlds, the investigators face random challenges and benefits.
- As gates open, a 'Doom Track' advances; if it reaches the end, a powerful horrific creature known as the Ancient One breaks through into Arkham.

Arkham Horror

The box cover of the revised edition of Arkham Horror

Players	1 to 8
Age range	12 and up
Setup time	30 to 60 minutes
Playing time	120 to 240 minutes
Random chance	Medium
Skill(s) required	Cooperative gaming

Chinese Checkers

- Despite its name, the game is not a variation of checkers, nor did it originate in China or any part of Asia.
- On the other hand, the game known as 'Chinese Chess', or Xiangqi, is from China.
- The game was invented in Germany in 1892 under

the name 'Stern-Halma' as a variation of the older American game Halma.

- The 'Stern' (German for star) refers to the board's star shape (in contrast to the square board used in Halma).

- The name 'Chinese Checkers' originated in the United States as a marketing scheme by Bill and Jack Pressman in 1928.

- The Pressman Company's game was originally called 'Hop Ching Checkers'.

- Six players can play this game at one time.

- Chinese checkers is a strategy board game which can be played by two, three, four or six people, playing individually or with partners.

- The game is a modern and simplified variation of the game Halma.

- The objective is to be the first to race one's pieces across the hexagram-shaped gameboard into 'home'—the destination corner of the star opposite one's starting corner—using single-step moves or moves which jump over other pieces.

- The others continue playing to establish 2nd, 3rd, 4th, 5th and last place.

- Like other skill-based games, Chinese checkers involves strategy. The rules are simple, so even young children can play.

- Each player has 10 pieces, except in games between

two players when 15 are sometimes used. (On bigger star boards, 15 or 21 pieces are used.)

❖ In 'hop across', the most popular variation, each player starts with their coloured pieces on one of the six points or corners of the star and attempts to race them all home into the opposite corner.

❖ Players take turns moving a single piece, either by moving one step in any direction to an adjacent empty space, or by jumping in one or any number of available consecutive hops over other single pieces.

❖ A player may not combine hopping with a single-step move—a move consists of one or the other.

❖ There is no capturing in Chinese checkers, so hopped pieces remain active and in play. Turns proceed clockwise around the board.

Chinese checkers

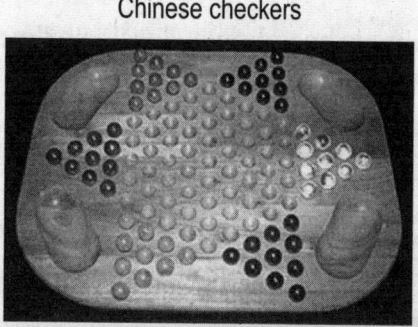

A typical pitted-wood gameboard using six differently coloured sets of marbles. Another popular arrangement uses differently coloured pegs in holes.

Genre(s)	Board game
	Abstract strategy game
Players	2 to 4 or 6
Age range	4+
Setup time	1 minute
Playing time	10 to 30 minutes
Random chance	None
Skill(s) required	Strategy, tactics
Synonym(s)	Star Halma
	Stern-Halma
	Hop Ching Checkers
	Tiau-qi (English: Jump chess)

Balderdash

❖ Balderdash is a board game of bluffing and trivia created by Lloyd Davies of south Wales.

❖ The game is based on a classic parlour game called Fictionary.

❖ The game was first released in 1984, under Canada Games.

❖ It was later picked up by a U.S company, The Games Gang, and eventually became the property of Hasbro, and finally Mattel.

❖ The game has sold over 15 million copies worldwide to date. It is aimed at fans of word games, such as Scrabble.

- The game begins by all players rolling a die, with the high roll chosen to be the first 'dasher'.
- The dasher draws a 'definition card' from the supplied box, and rolls the die to decide which of the words listed there is to be used.
- Then the dasher writes the definition of the word (as supplied on the card) on a piece of paper.
- All other players then write down a definition, which may be an honest attempt to supply the correct definition, or if they do not know or for tactical reasons decide not to, a fictitious definition for the word is designed to sound convincing.
- The players hand their definitions to the dasher.
- Players submitting the correct definition are immediately awarded three points, and if there is more than one, the round is abandoned (though the points are retained).
- The definitions, including the real definition, are then read out in random order.
- Players record which answer they believe is correct.
- Players are awarded two points if they guess the correct definition. Players are awarded one point for each other player who incorrectly chooses the fake definition they wrote. The dasher is awarded three points if no one guesses the correct definition. Players move their tokens around the game board one square for each point awarded. The role of dasher then passes to another player. The winner

is the individual whose token reaches the end square first.

✦✦✦✦✦✦

Axis and Allies

- ❖ Axis & Allies is a series of World War II strategy board games, with nearly two million copies printed.

- ❖ Originally designed by Larry Harris and published by Nova Game Designs in 1981, the game was republished by the Milton Bradley Company in 1984 as part of the Gamemaster Series of board games.

- ❖ The original Axis & Allies: Classic board game has been followed by ten spinoff games using more or less the same mechanics; in 1999, Axis & Allies: Europe was released, with slightly updated rules and focus on the European theatre of World War II; this was followed in 2001 by Axis & Allies: Pacific with similar rules and focus shifted to the Pacific theatre. Axis & Allies: D-Day (2004) focused on the Allied liberation of France.

❖ Axis & Allies is not a strict historical wargame, due to its streamlining for ease of play and balancing so that both sides have a chance to win. For instance, the economic model is simplistic, with each territory producing a number of Industrial Production Certificates (IPCs) for the purchase of new units. Moreover, the game is supposed to start in the spring of 1942, but Japan is immediately in position to attack Hawaii again, while Germany is pressed well into the Soviet Union with an initially superior force. If the game were truer to history, the Axis empires would be at their climax in 1942, about to be pushed back by the Allies.

Axis & Allies Board Game

Axis & Allies: Classic (1984)

Designer(s)	Larry Harris
Players	2 to 5
Age range	12+

Setup time	10 to 30 minutes
Playing time	2 to 10+ hours
Random chance	Medium
Skill(s) required	Tactics, strategy, economics, teamwork, logistics

Guess Who

- Guess Who is a two-player guessing game created by Ora and Theo Coster.
- It is also known as Theora Design.
- It was first manufactured by Milton Bradley in 1979 in Great Britain.
- It was brought to the United States in 1982.
- Each player starts the game with a board that includes cartoon images of 24 people and their first names with all the images standing up.
- The game starts with each player selecting a card from a separate pile of cards containing the same 24 images.
- The object of the game is to be the first to determine which card one's opponent has selected.
- Players alternate asking various yes or no questions to eliminate candidates, such as 'Does this person wear glasses?' The player will then eliminate candidates by flipping those images down until all

but one is left. Well-crafted questions allow players to eliminate one or more possible cards.

✦✦✦✦✦✦

Mouse Trap

- ❖ Mouse Trap (originally titled Mouse Trap Game) is a board game first published by Ideal in 1963 for 2 to 4 players.

- ❖ Once the mouse trap has been built, players turn against each other, attempting to trap opponents' mouse-shaped game pieces.

- ❖ The basic premise of the game has been consistent throughout the game's history. However, the turn-based gameplay has changed somewhat over the years.

- ❖ The original version allowed the players almost no decision-making, in keeping with other games for very young children such as Candyland or Chutes and Ladders (Snakes and Ladders).

❖ In the 1970s, the board game surrounding the Mouse Trap was redesigned by Sid Sackson, adding the cheese pieces and allowing the player to maneuver opponents onto the trap space.

❖ Another space on the board is the 'turn crank' space. Once the mouse trap is built, a player landing on one of these spaces while there is an opposing mouse on the 'cheese wheel' space must turn the crank to start the mouse trap.

❖ If you fold the board you can play a shorter game of Scene It.

❖ Not the 'diver' but the 'mouse' comes first in Mouse Trap.

Mouse Trap playing board and box.

BOARD & CARD GAMES

Players	2 to 4
Age range	6 +
Setup time	< 10 minutes
Playing time	30 minutes approx.
Random chance	High
Skill(s) required	Dice rolling, careful finger dexterity

II
DUNGEONS & DRAGONS

* Dungeons & Dragons was first published in 1974.
* It was Gary Gynax who co-created this game.
* Wizards of the Coast has been publishing this game since 1997.
* The Dungeon Master leads a game of Dungeons & Dragons.
* Dungeons & Dragons (abbreviated as D&D or DnD) is a fantasy tabletop role-playing game.
* It was derived from miniature wargames with a variation of the Chainmail game serving as the initial rule system.
* D&D's publication is widely regarded as the beginning of modern role-playing games and the role-playing game industry.
* It departs from traditional wargaming and assigns each player a specific character to play instead of a military formation.
* These characters embark upon imaginary adventures within a fantasy setting.
* A Dungeon Master serves as the game's referee and storyteller, while also maintaining the setting

in which the adventures occur and playing the role of the inhabitants.

- The characters form a party that interacts with the setting's inhabitants (and each other). Together they solve dilemmas, engage in battles and gather treasure and knowledge.
- In the process the characters earn experience points to become increasingly powerful over a series of sessions.
- Despite this competition, D&D remains the market leader in the role-playing game industry.
- In 1977, the game was split into two branches: the relatively rules-light game system of Dungeons & Dragons and the more structured, rules-heavy game system of Advanced Dungeons & Dragons (abbreviated as AD&D or ADnD).
- In Dungeons & Dragons, an NPC is a non-player character.
- Absent magical curses, three is the minimum score for ability.
- Absent magical enhancements, eighteen is the maximum score for ability.
- There was a Dungeons & Dragons movie.
- In this game, a D2O is a twenty-sided dice.
- TSR was the company that originally published Dungeons & Dragons.
- Paladin is the character class that shares its name

- with the lead character in the TV series Have Gun, Will Travel.
- Dead characters in Dungeons & Dragons can be revived.
- Oscar-winner Jeremy Iron starred in the movie Dungeons & Dragons.
- The magazine for Dungeons & Dragons enthusiasts is called The Dragon.
- There are nine possible character alignments.
- 'Chaotic-Evil' alignment is the polar opposite of 'Lawful-Good'.
- Monk character class is always true neutral.
- Magic Missiles spell is easier to learn than fireballs.
- Cleric character class is most useful against undead monsters.
- Tom Hanks, then a little known actor played the troubled student in a TV movie version of the Rona Jaffe novel.
- It is in Mazes and Monsters in Rona Jaffe novel that a troubled college student becomes dangerously obsessed with a Dungeons & Dragons-like game.
- A character's ability to withstand further attack is measured in Hit Points.
- Electrum pieces (coin) is more valuable than copper pieces but less valuable than silver pieces.

DUNGEONS & DRAGONS

4th Edition Dungeons & Dragons logo

Designer(s)	Gary Gygax Dave Arneson
Publisher(s)	TSR, Wizards of the Coast
Publication date	1974 (original) 1977 (D&D Basic Set 1st version) 1977–1979 (AD&D) 1981 (D&D Basic Set 2nd version) 1983–1986 (D&D Basic Set 3rd version) 1989 (AD&D 2nd Edition) 1991 (D&D Rules Cyclopedia) 2000 (D&D 3rd edition)[1] 2003 (D&D v3.5) 2008 (D&D 4th edition) 2014 (D&D 5th edition)
Years active	1974–present
Genre(s)	Fantasy
System(s)	Dungeons & Dragons d20 System (3rd Edition)
Playing time	Varies
Random chance	Dice rolling
Skill(s) required	Role-playing, improvisation, tactics, arithmetic
Website	wizards.com/dnd

✦✦✦✦✦✦

III
SCRABBLE

- There are nine A tiles in a game of Scrabble.
- Scrabble's original name was Lexicon.
- Its creator was named Alfred Butts.
- The same inventor created a game called Alfred's Other Game.
- There is no scrabble-acceptable two-letter word containing a U.
- The rule change in Duplicate Scrabble is that all players play with the same letter.
- It is not possible to play scrabble with Chinese letters.
- In French Scrabble, the X and the Y are each worth 10 points.
- There are fifteen wide spaces on a Scrabble board.
- Scrabble is an acceptable Scrabble word.
- You get fifty extra points for using all seven of your letters in one play in Scrabble.
- Scrabble tiles are made from Vermont maple.
- Scrabble was originally played without a board.

- An M is worth three points in a game of Scrabble.
- The word quizzical is impossible to get in scrabble without using a blank because there is only one Z.
- In determining which player goes first in scrabble, a blank tile beats an A tile.
- The highest possible opening word in scrabble is Muzjiks. One would get 128 points (keeping in mind that the opener uses a double word square).
- In scrabble are there more Fs than Ks.
- There are more Ds than Bs.
- There more Us than Ps.
- There more Gs than Vs.
- There are more acceptable Scrabble words containing a Q than those containing a U.
- Five letters are represented just once in a set.
- There are 100 tiles in a Scrabble set.
- A losing player at the World Scrabble Championship once accused his opponent of pocketing a G and demanded that officials strip-search him.
- National Scrabble Championship officials once disallowed a word because it was considered offensive, even though it was in the dictionary.
- Word Wars is a documentary that chronicles championship-level Scrabble players.

Latest information:

❖ The resource which publishes the official dictionary for the World English language Scrabble Players Association recently approved 6,500 new words.

❖ Slang words like 'beehive' which is a bad hairdo, 'Lolz' and 'Thanx' have been included.

❖ The World Scrabble Championship was held in Melbourne.

❖ We now have teenager vocabulary: Eew, eeew.

Former Scrabble brand logo, used worldwide by Mattel outside U.S. and Canada until 2013

Scrabble logo used by Hasbro within U.S. and Canada until 2014

Manufacturer(s)	Mattel (outside U.S. and Canada) Hasbro (within U.S. and Canada)
Designer(s)	Alfred Mosher Butts
Publisher(s)	James Brunot
Publication date	1938; 77 years ago

SCRABBLE

Genre(s)	Word game Board game
Players	2 to 4
Age range	8+
Setup time	2 to 6 minutes
Playing time	NASPA tournament game: 50 minutes
Random chance	Medium (letters drawn)
Skill(s) required	Vocabulary, spelling, anagramming, strategy, counting, bluffing, probability

IV
RISK

- ❖ The man who invented Risk, Albert Lamorisse, was a French film director who also made the award-winning film The Red Balloon. The movie came in 1956 and the game came a year later.
- ❖ Risk is the potential of losing something of value.
- ❖ Values (such as physical health, social status, emotional well being or financial wealth) can be gained or lost when taking risk resulting from a given action, activity and/or inaction, foreseen or unforeseen.
- ❖ Risk can also be defined as the intentional interaction with uncertainty.
- ❖ Uncertainty is a potential, unpredictable, unmeasurable and uncontrollable outcome; risk is a consequence of an action taken in spite of uncertainty.
- ❖ Risk perception is the subjective judgment people make about the severity and/or probability of a risk, and may vary person to person.

- Any human endeavour carries some risk, but some are much riskier than others.
- Asia is the continent that has the most territories.
- If you have six attacking armies and your opponent has six defending armies, you have 52 per cent chances of winning the battle.
- There are eight continents on the Risk board.
- If two players are playing, each player starts with 40 armies.
- Generally, continents with fewer borders are easier to defend as they possess fewer points that can be attacked by other players. South America has 2 access points, North America and Africa each have 3, Europe has 4 and Asia has 5.
- You must have two armies in order to take hold of a neighbouring country.
- The current rules for two-player Risk weren't incorporated into the official game until 1945.
- Venezuela is a territory in Risk.
- Quebec is a territory.
- Italy is not a territory.
- Iceland cannot attack Ukraine.
- Egypt cannot attack Congo.

- ❖ The Middle East is not a part of Africa but Asia.
- ❖ Castle Risk focuses only on the continent of Europe.

✦✦✦✦✦✦

V
THE GAME OF LIFE

- ❖ An early version of the Game of Life was called the Checkered Game of Life.

- ❖ The Game of Life, also known simply as Life, is a board game originally created in 1860 by Milton Bradley.

- ❖ The Game of Life was America's first popular parlour game.

- ❖ The game simulates a person's travels through his or her life, from college to retirement, with jobs, marriage, and possible children along the way.

- ❖ Two to six players can participate in one game.

- ❖ Variations of the game accommodate eight to ten players.

- ❖ The modern version was originally published 100 years later, in 1960.

- ❖ It was created by toy and game designer Reuben Klamerand and endorsed by Art Linkletter.

- ❖ It is now part of the permanent collection of the Smithsonian's National Museum of American History.

- It later spawned a book, The Game of Life: How to Succeed in Real Life No Matter Where You Land (Running Press), by Lou Harry.
- The contemporary version of the Game of Life was first released in 1960.
- There are ten numbers on the spinner.
- The $500 bills have been dropped from the game.
- One cannot buy renter's insurance in this game.
- One can buy flood insurance though.
- One can buy life insurance also.
- In the 1960's edition, you could end up at the Poor Farm.
- The original Game of Life cars were convertibles.
- In the early editions of the game, Art Linkletter appeared on its cover.
- Life Tiles, which rewarded good behaviour, was added in the 1990s.
- There are six peg holes in a Game of Life car. Some editions have eight.

	The Game of Life
Designer(s)	Reuben Klamer Bill Markham
Publisher(s)	Milton Bradley Company and Winning Moves
Players	2 to 6

THE GAME OF LIFE

Age range	9 to adult
Setup time	10 minutes (approx.)
Playing time	45 minutes (approx.)
Random chance	High (spinning a wheel, card-drawing, luck)
Skill(s) required	Counting, reading

VI
CLUE

- Cluedo, or Clue in North America, is a murder mystery game for three to six players.

- It was devised by Anthony E. Pratt from Birmingham, England and is currently published by the United States game and toy company Hasbro.

- The object of the game is to determine who murdered the game's victim ('Dr. Black' in the UK version and 'Mr. Boddy' in North American versions), where the crime took place, and which weapon was used.

- Each player assumes the role of one of the six suspects, and attempts to deduce the correct answer by strategically moving around a game board representing the rooms of a mansion and collecting clues about the circumstances of the murder from the other players.

- Numerous games, books and a film have been released as part of the Cluedo franchise.

- Several spinoffs have been released featuring various extra characters, weapons and rooms, or different game play.

- The original game is marketed as the 'Classic Detective Game', while the various spinoffs are all distinguished by different slogans.
- The game consists of a board which shows the rooms, corridors and secret passages of an English country house called Tudor Mansion, although previously named variously as Tudor Close or Tudor Hall, and in some editions Boddy Manor or Boddy Mansion.
- The game box also includes several coloured playing pieces to represent characters, miniature murder weapon props, one or two six-sided dice, three sets of cards, each set describing the rooms, characters and weapons, Solution Cards envelope to contain one card from each set of cards, and a Detective's Notes pad on which are printed lists of rooms, weapons and characters, so players can keep detailed notes during the game.
- Colonel Mustard is the name of the colonel in Clue.
- In England, the game is known as Cluedo.
- The blue colour piece is Mrs Peacock.
- In the British edition of Clue, Mr Green is Rev Green.
- In some editions of the game, the rope is made of string. In others, it's plastic.
- If you accuse another player of being the killer, his piece is automatically moved into the room you are in.

- 324 possible murderer/location/weapon combination are there in a standard game.
- You are allowed to block a room to prevent another player from entering.
- When it was released in theatre, the movie Clue had different endings that could change from screening to screening.
- In Clue, we have Dining Room, Kitchen and Conservatory. But there is no Laundry Room.
- A bottle of poison was the extra murder weapon in the 50th anniversary edition of Clue.
- Mr Burns is the victim in the Simpsons Clue.
- Mrs White's piece starts closest to the Ballroom.
- A Clue-like game in which players wander a mansion trying to kill a character rather than find the murderer is called Kill Dr Lucky.
- The Billiard room does not have a secret passageway.
- The Ballroom has the most doors.
- Miss Scarlet is the player who goes first.
- Prof Plum is the character who goes last.
- Detective Notes is the heading on the pads for you to keep track of your deductions.

Cluedo/Clue

Designer(s)	Anthony E. Pratt
Publisher(s)	Waddingtons Parker Brothers Hasbro Winning Moves
Players	2 to 6 3 to 6 (editions vary)
Age range	8 and up
Setup time	5 minutes
Playing time	15 to 60 minutes
Random chance	Low (dice rolling)
Skill(s) required	Deduction

VII
MONOPOLY

- By 1933, a variation on 'The Landlord's Game' called Monopoly was the basis of the board game sold by Parker Brothers, beginning on 6 February 1935.

- Monopoly is a board game that originated in the United States in 1903 as a way to demonstrate that an economy which rewards wealth creation is better than one in which monopolists work under few constraints.

- This was to promote the economic theories of Henry George and in particular his ideas about taxation and women's rights.

- The current version was first published by Parker Brothers in 1935.

- Subtitled 'The Fast-Dealing Property Trading Game', the game is named after the economic concept of monopoly—the domination of a market by a single entity.

- It is now produced by the United States game and toy company Hasbro.

- Players move around the gameboard buying or trading properties, developing their properties with houses and hotels, and collecting rent from their opponents, with the goal being to drive them all into bankruptcy leaving one monopolist in control of the entire economy.

- ❖ Since the board game was first commercially sold in the 1930s, it has become a part of popular world culture, with it being locally licensed in more than 103 countries and printed in more than 37 languages.
- ❖ Mediterranean and Baltic are the first two purchasable properties on the Monopoly board.
- ❖ Reading, B&O, Short Line, Pennsylvania are the four Monopoly railroads.
- ❖ 'You've won second prize in a beauty contest' is not a Chance card but a Community Chest card.
- ❖ The rich Uncle Pennybags character, best known from Monopoly, also appeared on Careers.
- ❖ A Monopoly game contains more than $12,000 in play money.
- ❖ Monopoly is available in more than 40 languages.
- ❖ The longest recorded Monopoly game lasted more than 70 days.
- ❖ A jeweller created a version of the game valued at $2 million.
- ❖ In Spain, the Broadway space has been replaced with Paseo del Prado.

- Escape maps were hidden in Monopoly sets that were sent to American prisoners of war during World War II.
- The person in Monopoly jail has an official name: Jake, the Jailbird.
- In the movie Zombie, the characters play Monopoly with real money.
- The prize at the Monopoly World Championships is the real dollar equivalent of the amount of fake money in a Monopoly game box.
- $20,580 is the amount of money in a Monopoly game box.
- There's a version of Monopoly with round boards.
- Twenty-eight properties are there in a Monopoly game.
- The cost of the luxury tax has changed in Monopoly.
- The real B&O railroad did not serve Atlantic city.
- You get $200 for passing Go in regular Monopoly.
- The World Monopoly Tournament has been aired on ESPN.
- A top hat is a Monopoly playing piece.
- There are two utilities in a Monopoly game.
- There are twelve hotels and thirty-two houses in a Monopoly game.
- The $20 bills are blue in colour.

MONOPOLY

- ❖ The $1 bills are white in colour.
- ❖ While in jail, you can buy undeveloped property from another player for its face value.
- ❖ Rich Uncle Pennybags officially had his name changed to Mr. Monopoly by Parker Brothers.
- ❖ Each player starts with $1500.
- ❖ If you roll nothing but sevens the entire game, the only property you will never land on is Park Palace.
- ❖ In British Monopoly, the Income Tax space is called 'Luxury Tax'.
- ❖ If you have three hotels and nine houses, and you are assessed for street repairs, you owe $705.
- ❖ Only two monopolies consist of just two properties.
- ❖ Illinois Avenue is the space on the board that is landed on the most.
- ❖ An economics professor trying to illustrate the virtues of a free market over monopolies, published a game called Anti-Monopoly.
- ❖ Monopoly was banned in the Soviet Union as capitalistic.
- ❖ Charles Darrow invented Monopoly and there is evidence that he copied an earlier game.
- ❖ There are nine Monopoly properties that you can reach by drawing a chance card.

- Parker Brothers was the first company to mass-market Monopoly.
- If you get out of jail by throwing doubles, you do not get an extra turn.
- There are two Monopoly properties that are named after saints.
- Not counting the railroads and utilities, there are seven properties that are neither states nor bodies of water.
- You get $200 plus 2 in Whoville-Opoly for passing Go.
- States Avenue is the property that completes the Monopoly if you own St Charles Place and Virginia Ave.
- Ventnor Ave is the property that completes the Monopoly if you own Marvin Gardens and Atlantic Ave.
- St James Avenue is the property that completes the Monopoly if you own North Carolina and Pennsylvania Avenues.
- Kentucky Avenue is the property that completes the Monopoly if you own Illinois and Indiana Avenues.
- St James Avenue is the property that completes the Monopoly if you own New York and Tennessee Avenues.

Monopoly
The Fast-Dealing Property Trading Game

The Monopoly logo (2009–present)

Designer(s)	Elizabeth Magie Charles Darrow
Illustrator(s)	Matt Pocock
Publisher(s)	Hasbro Parker Brothers Waddingtons
Players	Some versions 2 to 6 Other versions 2 to 8
Setup time	5 to 10 minutes
Playing time	60 to 240 minutes (1 to 4 hours) [average]
Random chance	High (dice rolling, card drawing)
Skill(s) required	Negotiation Resource management Strategy

VIII
PUZZLES

KenKen

- Kenken was invented by a math teacher.
- In a Crossword puzzle, across clues are usually listed first as opposed to the down clues.
- A Crossword creator is a cruciverbalist.
- The American-style puzzle Crossword grid has more letter squares in a same style size than a British-style Crossword grid.
- KenKen and KenDoku are trademarked names for a style of arithmetic and logic puzzle invented in 2004 by Japanese math teacher Tetsuya Miyamoto.
- He intended the puzzle to be an instruction-free method of training the brain.
- The names Calcudoku and Mathdoku are sometimes used by those who don't have the rights to use the KenKen or KenDoku trademarks.
- The name derives from the Japanese word for cleverness.
- As in Sudoku, the goal of each puzzle is to fill a grid with digits—1 through 4 for a 4×4 grid, 1 through 5

for a 5×5, etc.—so that no digit appears more than once in any row or any column (a Latin square).

- Grids range in size from 3×3 to 9×9.
- Additionally, KenKen grids are divided into heavily outlined groups of cells—often called 'cages'—and the numbers in the cells of each cage must produce a certain 'target' number when combined using a specified mathematical operation (either addition, subtraction, multiplication or division).
- For example, a linear three-cell cage specifying addition and a target number of 6 in a 4×4 puzzle must be satisfied with the digits 1, 2 and 3. Digits may be repeated within a cage, as long as they are not in the same row or column. No operation is relevant for a single-cell cage: placing the 'target' in the cell is the only possibility (thus being a 'free space'). The target number and operation appear in the upper left-hand corner of the cage.
- In the English-language KenKen books of Will Shortz, the issue of the non-associativity of division and subtraction is addressed by restricting clues based on either of those operations to cages of only two cells in which the numbers may appear in any order. Hence if the target is 1 and the operation is—(subtraction) and the number choices are 2 and 3, possible answers are 2, 3 or 3, 2. Some puzzle authors have not done this and have published puzzles that use more than two cells for these operations.

Sudoku

- The first World Sudoku Championship was held in Italy.
- There are 81 small squares in a standard Sudoku puzzle.
- Nine is the highest number in a standard Sudoku puzzle.
- While its origins are vague, the modern Sudoku puzzle format is believed to have been created by Howard Garns of Indiana.
- Nikoli was the company that first popularized Sudoku puzzles in 1986.
- Six numbers are used in mini Sudoku.
- When a Sudoku puzzle first appeared in the British newspaper The Times, it was called Su Doku.
- The Sky One TV show Sudoku Live featured nine players on nine teams.

5	3			7				
6			1	9	5			
	9	8					6	
8				6				3
4			8		3			1
7				2				6
	6					2	8	
			4	1	9			5
				8			7	9

Crossword puzzles

- In a Japanese Crossword puzzle, the corners are traditionally all white squares.
- In Japanese Crossword puzzles, no two shaded squares are next to or on top of each other.
- In a Crossword puzzle, a question mark is used to indicate that the clue indicates a pun.
- An abbreviation in a clue indicates the answer is in abbreviated form.
- The first Crossword puzzle was published in 1890.
- The first Crossword puzzle book was published in 1924.
- It was in 1942 that the New York Times began publishing Crossword puzzles.
- The first 30 American Crossword Puzzle Tournaments were held in Stanford, Connecticut.
- William Shertz, founded the American Crossword Puzzle Tournament.
- Word Search Puzzles were first published in the 1960s.

Jigsaw puzzles

- More Jigsaw puzzles are made of cardboard than wood.
- All 1,000-piece Jigsaw puzzles do not have the same pattern of pieces, only with different illustrations.

- The company Ravensburger created a Jigsaw puzzle of over 18,000 pieces.
- Many 1,000-piece Jigsaw puzzles actually have more than 1,000 pieces.
- The oldest Jigsaw puzzle—then called a dissected puzzle—was created by a London mapmaker.
- Early Jigsaw puzzles were actually cut by a fretsaw, not a jigsaw.
- During the Great Depression, there were companies that issued weekly Jigsaw puzzles.

IX
PLAYGROUND & BACKYARD GAMES

- ❖ The Four Square World Championship is held in Maryland.
- ❖ Students at Manchester college played Four Square for 120 hours to set a world record in 1960s.
- ❖ In competitive Four Square, you are allowed to spin the ball on a serve.
- ❖ In Four Square, a ball that bounces on a line is in.
- ❖ The server in the game serves from the highest ranking square.
- ❖ Your feet do not have to stay in your square.
- ❖ In Hopscotch, a marker has to be completely in the numbered area.
- ❖ In Chain Tag, when he or she tags someone, they hold hands with the new 'It' person, forming a lengthening chain.
- ❖ In Zombie Tag (aka Gang Up or Minion Tag) when a person is tagged, the tagger says, 'Tag, you're it'.
- ❖ In Duck Duck Goose, you get up and chase if you are tapped and called a goose.

- In Freeze Tag, you are unfrozen when someone who has not tagged, tags you.
- The balls are lined up in centre court up at the beginning of a game of Dodgeball.
- In Dodgeball, if you catch a ball thrown at you, the thrower is eliminated.
- In 2011, a game of Dodgeball at the University of California, Irvine, included more than 4,400 players.
- Aggie, Mica and Cat's Eye are all types of marbles.
- Wickets is another name for Croquet hoops.
- In a standard game of Croquet, if your ball hits someone else's ball you get two more shots.
- You get more shots when your ball goes through the correct wicket.
- There are nine wickets in a standard backyard game of Croquet.
- It is generally better to go last in Croquet.
- You have to go through wickets in order.
- In Croquet, the person whose turn it is is called the 'Striker'.
- Three points are awarded for a ringer in Horseshoes.
- A live shoe that is not a ringer, but comes to rest 6 inches or closer to the stake, has a value of one point.

- The other name for a close shoe in Horseshoes is a Shoe count.
- A contestant observing the thirty–seven-foot foul line may start directly behind the platform provided they step within it when they release the shoe.
- The steel rod should be 14 inches above the ground to play this game.
- Horseshoe stakes are supposed to lean toward the tosser.
- Hooked ends took the place of pointed ends in this game in 1955.
- Bocce comes from the Latin meaning 'boss'.
- Romans sometimes used coconuts to play an early version of Bocce.
- King Carlos IV and King Carlos V of Spain were the two kings to prohibit Bocce playing.
- There are three games in a Bocce match.
- In Championship Bocce, the first is three-on-three, the second is one-on-one, and the third is two-on-two, with no players playing more than twice.
- The Championship Bocce game usually goes to fifteen points.
- One team always gets zero in a round of Bocce, because only the highest-scoring team gets points.
- The name of the small ball in Bocce is Pallino.

- In International Bocce, there are punto, raffa and volo shots.
- An official Bocce ball weighs between 9800-1200 grams.
- Kickball was originally called Kick Baseball.
- Kickball has been played since around 1917.
- In early Kickball, there was no pitcher.
- The traditional Kickball ball is red.
- According to WAKA, between 8 and 11 players are needed on a Kickball team.
- Between a playground game, Kickball rules adapt to location and region. But according to the World Adult Kickball Association, the distance between the strike zone at home and second base should be 84 feet.
- According to WAKA, fifteen innings makes a full Kickball game.
- You need three points to get in Cornhole for landing a bag in the hole.
- You will get one point in Cornhole for landing a bag on the platform.
- You need twenty-one points to win a game of Cornhole.
- You need four bags to throw in an inning of Cornhole.
- There are three rungs on each ladder in a game of Ladder.

- In Ladder Toss, the top rung is worth three points.
- In Ladder Toss (aka Ladder Golf and Hillbilly Golf), the strung-together balls are called bolas.
- One bola on each rung or three bolas on the same rung are the two ways of getting a bonus point in Ladder Toss.
- Wiffle Ball was invented in the 1950s.
- There are eight holes in a standard Wiffle Ball.
- Curve, straight and sliders are the three basic pitches in Wiffle Ball.
- In Wiffle Ball, if a ball is caught in the air in fair territory, it's considered an out.
- You don't need bases in an official Wiffle Ball game.

✦✦✦✦✦✦

X
VIDEO GAMES

- A video game is an electronic game that involves human interaction with a user interface to generate visual feedback on a video device.

- The word video in video game traditionally referred to a raster display device.

- Now it implies any type of display device that can produce two- or three-dimensional images.

- The electronic systems used to play video games are known as platforms; examples of these are personal computers and video game consoles.

- These platforms range from large mainframe computers to small handheld devices.

- Specialised video games such as arcade games, while previously common, have gradually declined in use.

- The input device used for games, a game controller, varies across platforms.

- Common controllers include gamepads, mouses, keyboards, joysticks and the touchscreens of mobile devices.

- In addition to video and (in most cases) audio feedback, some games include haptic, vibration or force feedback peripherals.
- Video games have become an art form and an industry.
- The video game industry is of increasing commercial importance, with growth driven particularly by the emerging Asian markets and mobile games.
- As of 2015, video games generated sales of USD 74 billion annually worldwide, and were the third-largest segment in the US entertainment market, behind broadcast and cable TV.
- Early games used interactive electronic devices with various display formats. The earliest example is from 1947—a 'Cathode ray tube Amusement Device' was filed for a patent on 25 January 1947, by Thomas T. Goldsmith Jr and Estle Ray Mann, and issued on 14 December 1948, as US Patent.

Platforms

- The term 'platform' refers to the specific combination of electronic components or computer hardware which, in conjunction with software, allows a video game to operate.
- The term 'system' is also commonly used.

- In common use, a 'PC game' refers to a form of media that involves a player interacting with a personal computer connected to a video monitor.
- A 'console game' is played on a specialised electronic device that connects to a common television set or composite video monitor.
- A 'handheld' gaming device is a self-contained electronic device that is portable and can be held in a user's hands.
- 'Arcade game' generally refers to a game played on an even more specialized type of electronic device that is typically designed to play only one game and is encased in a special cabinet.
- In addition to personal computers, there are multiple other devices which have the ability to play games but are not dedicated video game machines, such as mobile phones, PDAs and graphing calculators.
- The web browser has also established itself as a platform in its own right while providing a cross-platform environment for video games designed to be played on a wide spectrum of hardware from personal computers to smartphones to name a few.
- This, in turn, has generated new terms to qualify classes of web browser based games.
- These games may be identified based on the websites that they appear in, such as with 'Facebook' games.

- ❖ Others are named based on the programming platform used to develop them, such as Java and Flash games.

Classifications

Casual Games

- ❖ Casual games derive their name from their ease of accessibility, simple to understand gameplay and quick to grasp rule sets.
- ❖ Additionally, casual games frequently support the ability to jump in and out of play on demand.
- ❖ Casual games, as a format, existed long before the term was coined and include video games such as Solitaire or Minesweeper which can commonly be found pre-installed with many versions of the Microsoft Windows operating system.
- ❖ Examples of genres within this category are match three, hidden object, time management, puzzle or many of the tower defense style games.
- ❖ Casual games are generally available through app stores and online retailers such as PopCap, Zylom and GameHouse or provided for free play through web portals such as Newgrounds.

Serious Games

- ❖ Serious games are games that are designed primarily to convey information or a learning experience of some sort to the player.

- ❖ Some serious games may even fail to qualify as a video game in the traditional sense of the term.
- ❖ Educational software does not typically fall under this category (e.g. touch typing tutors, language learning, etc.).
- ❖ Serious games are games generally made for reasons beyond simple entertainment and may include works from any given genre, although some such as exergames, educational games or propaganda games may have a higher representation in this group due to their subject matter.
- ❖ These games are typically designed to be played by professionals as part of a specific job or for skill set improvement. They can also be created to convey social-political awareness on a specific subject.
- ❖ One of the longest running serious games franchises would be Microsoft Flight Simulator, first published in 1982 under that name.
- ❖ The United States military uses virtual reality based simulations, such as VBS1 for training exercises, as do a growing number of first responder roles (e.g. police, fire fighter, EMT).

Educational Games

- ❖ On 23 September 2009, US President Barack Obama launched a campaign called 'Educate to Innovate' aimed at improving the technological, mathematical, scientific and engineering abilities of American students.

- This campaign states that it plans to harness the power of interactive games to help achieve the goal of students excelling in these departments.
- This campaign has stemmed into many new opportunities for the video game realm and has contributed to many new competitions.
- Some of these competitions include the Stem National Video Game Competition and the Imagine Cup.
- Both of these examples are events that bring focus to relevant and important current issues that are able to be addressed in the sense of video games to educate and spread knowledge in a new form of media.
- www.NobelPrize.org uses games to entice the user to learn about information pertaining to the Nobel prize achievements while engaging in a video game.
- There are many different types and styles of educational games all the way from counting to spelling to games for kids and games for adults.
- Some other games do not have any particular targeted audience in mind and intend to simply educate or inform whoever views or plays the game.

Cheating

- ❖ Cheating in computer games may involve cheat codes and hidden spots implemented by the game developers, modification of game code by third parties or players exploiting a software glitch.
- ❖ Modifications are facilitated by either cheat cartridge hardware or a software trainer.
- ❖ Cheats usually make the game easier by providing an unlimited amount of some resource; for example weapons, health or ammunition; or perhaps the ability to walk through walls.
- ❖ Other cheats might give access to otherwise unplayable levels or provide unusual or amusing features, like altered game colours or other graphical appearances.
- ❖ The Magnavox Odyssey was the first home video game system.
- ❖ Atari is a term used when playing GO.
- ❖ It was in the year 1978 that space invaders first invaded Arcades.
- ❖ Sears was the exclusive seller of Atari Pong's game.
- ❖ Teris is the name of the addictive game developed by Russian programmer Alex Pajitnov in 1985.
- ❖ It was in the year 1989 that the Nintendo game boy first released.
- ❖ Asteroids came first, before Pac-Man.

VIDEO GAMES

- The Entertainment Software Ratings Board began in 1994, the same year that the Sony PlayStation was launched in Japan.
- Tamagotchi came first, then Sims.
- Sony PSP came first, then Nintendo's Wii.
- Super Mario Bros 3 came before Super Mario World.
- Super Mario Bros is a spin-off from the game Donkey Kong.
- The first John Madden Football Game was designed for Apple II.
- The original Guitar Hero was released for PlayStation 2.
- Pink and blue are two colours of the arrow footpads on the standard Dance Dance Revolution Arcade Game.
- Myst came first, then Halo.
- The Nintendo entertainment system was first known as Famicon.
- The highest possible score in Pac-Man is 3,333,360.
- A 1982 song called 'Pac-Man Fever' actually became a top-10 record.
- Pac-Man is yellow in colour.
- Pac-Man games sold more copies than Atari, Missile Command.

The Villains in Video Games

Giados	Portal
Mother Brain	Metroid Games
Bowser	Mario Games
Andrew Ryan	Bioshock
Ganon	Zelda Games
Dr Robotnik	Sonic The Hedgehog Games
Dr Willy	Mega Man Games
Albert Weske	Resident Evil Games
M. Bison	Street Fighter Games
Joker	Batman Games
Covenant	Halo
Lich King	World Of Warcraft
Gru	Zork
Zeus	God Of War Series
Captain Qwark	Ratchet And Clank Games

- In Sims, being a getaway driver gets you more money than being a con artist.
- In Sims, being a counterfeiter gets you more money than being a bank robber.
- In Sims, being a smuggler gets you more money than being a cat burglar.
- Sims live in SimCity.
- In the first Sims game, children did not grow up into adults.
- After a sim dies, it may haunt the place where its life ended.
- When it was released, The Sims became the bestselling game in PC history.
- The Sims spoke Simlish.
- The Sims: House Party came before The Sims: Vacation.
- The Sims: Hot Date came before The Sims: Superstar.
- Wii Fit sold more copies than Mario Party 8.
- Wii Party sold more copies than Wii Play.
- Over $2.5 billion in quarters were spent on Pac-Man video games.
- Wii Sports sold more than Super Mario Galaxy.
- For PlayStation: Tomb Raider II sold more than Tom Raider.

- Grand Theft Auto III sold more for PlayStation 2 than Final Fantasy X.
- The Wii was available in white in its first year.
- Revolution was the code name for the Wii while it was in development.
- Super Mario Indestructible was not a Super Mario game for Wii.

The Title of Wii Games

Active life	: Extreme Challenge
Alien Monster Bowling League	
AMF Bowling World Lanes	
Are You Smarter Than a 5th grader	: Make the Grade
Backyard Sports	: Sandlot Slugger
Batman	: The Brave and the Bold
Big Brain Academy	: Wii Degree
Bratz	: Girlz Really Rock!
Cabela's Big Game Hunter	
Call of Duty	: Black Ops
Celebrity Sports Showdown	
Doctor Fizzwhizzle's Animal Rescue	
Donkey Kong Jungle Beat	
Kidz Bop Dance Party	
Kirby's Return to Dreamland	
Legend of Zelda; Skyward Sword	
Mario and Sonic at the Olympic Games	
My Sims	: Sky Heroes
Pet Pals	: Animal Doctor
Pirates vs. Ninjas	: Dodgeball

- Wii: LEGO Batman came before LEGO Harry Potter.
- The designer of Angry Birds is from Finland.
- In Angry Birds, a player tries to hit the birds with pigs.
- The birds at the initial levels of Angry Birds are red in colour.
- Three smaller birds can be separated by the blue bird in Angry Birds.
- There are twenty-one levels in each chapter of the initial release of Angry Birds.
- Rovio, the maker of Angry Birds, also made the game Desert Sniper.
- Russia invades the US in Call of Duty: Modern Warfare 3.
- According to Portal 2, the game is set in Michigan.
- The player character in Portal is promised cakes as a prize when all of the puzzles are solved.
- Chell is the name of the player character in Portal.
- In Portal, GLaDOS stands for Genetic Lifeform and Disk Operating System.
- The Legend of Zelda was originally released as the Hyrule Fantasy: Legend of Zelda.
- In Zelda, there are eight fragments of the Triforce of wisdom to be collected.

- Zelda takes place in the land of Hyrule.
- Link is the boy hero in the legend of Zelda.
- Ganon is the villain of the Legend of Zelda.
- Impa is Zelda's nursemaid's name.

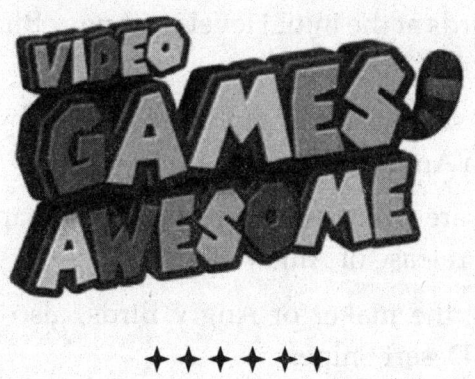

✦✦✦✦✦✦

XI
TRADITIONAL GAMES OF INDIA

Some of the traditional games in India are Kabaddi, Goli, Ghilli or the indoor games like the Dhaayakattam, Paramapadham, Pallanguzhi, Paandi or Aadu Puli Aattam.

These games have a rich culture and heritage value and were tools of passing on some ancestral knowledge or the other.

They also sharpened our observational and math skills unlike the hit-and-run games of the west that are uni-dimensional and strengthen only hand-eye coordination.

Gutte

This traditional game is played by both children and adults. This simple game requires 5 pieces of small stones. You spin one stone in the air and pick other stones from the ground without dropping the stone in the air. This game can be played by any number of people.

Kancha

Kancha is one of the most popular games among children in the neighbourhood. It is played using marbles called 'kancha'. The players are to hit the selected target 'kancha' using their own marble ball. The winner takes all kanchas of rest of the players.

Kho Kho

It is one of the most popular tag games in India. It consists of two teams. One team sits/kneels in the middle of the court, in a row, with adjacent members facing opposite directions. The team that takes the shortest time to tag/tap all the opponents in the field wins.

Gilli Danda

The game requires two sticks. The bigger one is called 'danda' and the smaller one is called 'gilli'. The player then uses the danda to hit the gilli at the raised end, which flips it into the air. While it is in the air, the player strikes the gilli, hitting it as far as possible. Having struck the gilli, the player is required to run and touch a pre-agreed point outside the circle before the gilli is retrieved by an opponent.

Poshampa

Two people stand with their hands locked together

above their heads and sing a song. The other kids pass from under that bridge and the one who gets caught (when the hands come down like a cage at the end of the song) is out.

Chaupa/Pachis

Each player's objective is to move all four of his/her pieces completely around the board, counter-clockwise, before the opponent does. The pieces start and finish on the Charkoni.

Kith Kith

A popular playground game in which players toss a small object into numbered spaces of a pattern of rectangles outlined on the ground and then hop or jump through the spaces to retrieve the object. This popular game is also played in other countries and is loved by all.

DhopKhel

DhopKhel, a game popular in Assam, is similar to Kabbadi. Dhop is the name given to a rubber ball that two teams throw across a central line into each other's courts. Each team sends a player into the opponent's court; the aim is to catch the ball his team throws and make his way back to his team without allowing the opponents to touch him to earn points.

Pallanguli

This board game with 14 cups is set out with six seeds in each cup; the players distribute these seeds into the other cups until there are no seeds left. The person who reaches two consecutive cups without seeds has to bow out of the game.

Satoliya

- ❖ The game is also called *Pithoo* or *Lagori* in some parts of India. It is generally played between two teams in a large outdoor area. It needs seven small flat stones; every stone size should be less than the other stone. The stones are kept on each other in an ascending order. A member of one team (the seekers) throws a soft ball at a pile of stones to knock them over. The seekers then try to restore the pile of stones while the opposing team (the hitters) throws the ball at them. If the ball touches a seeker, he is out and his team continues without him. But a team member can always safeguard himself by touching the opposite team member before the ball hits him.

New Islamic Fun Games

- ❖ These set of new games are meant to help kids not get addicted to the Internet. Concept: learn and play.

- ❖ Games like 'Quran Challenge', 'Haj Fun Games' and 'Ramdan Fun Pack' are a few examples.
- ❖ They are played with dice, cards, spinning wheel and styled in the conventional Ludo, and Snake and Ladder format.
- ❖ In 'Hadith Challenge' there are questions and answers in a card.

✦✦✦✦✦✦